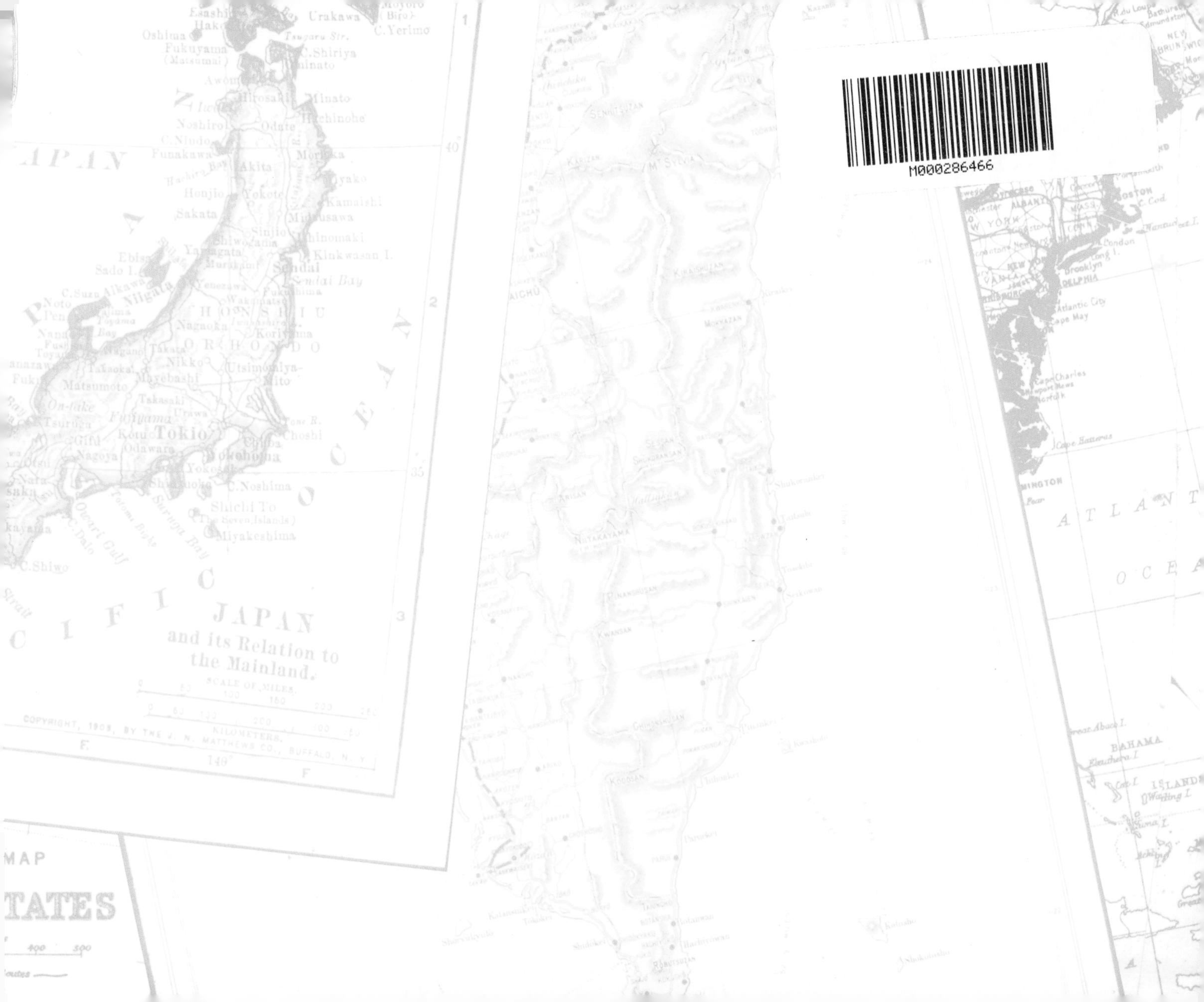
JAPAN
and its Relation to the Mainland.
SCALE OF MILES
KILOMETERS
COPYRIGHT, 1903, BY THE J. N. MATTHEWS CO., BUFFALO, N. Y.
PACIFIC OCEAN
HONSHIU OR HONDO
Tokio
Yokohama
Sendai
Niigata
Akita
Hakodate
Fukuyama
Hirosaki
Morioka
Miyako
Kamaishi
Sakata
Honjio
Yokote
Yamagata
Nagoya
Gifu
Tsuruga
Shizuoka
Chiba
Choshi
Nikko
Mito
Takasaki
Odawara
Fujiyama
Sado I.
Kinkwasan I.
Shichi To
(The Seven Islands)
Miyakeshima
C. Noshima
C. Shiwo
Sagami Bay
Owari Gulf
Totomi Bight
Sendai Bay
MAP
TATES
ATLANTIC
OCEAN
BOSTON
C. Cod
NEW YORK
Brooklyn
Atlantic City
Cape May
Cape Charles
Norfolk
Cape Hatteras
BAHAMA
ISLANDS
Great Abaco I.
Eleuthera I.
Cat I.
Watling I.

The Whyte Museum of the Canadian Rockies Presents

AN ADVENTUROUS WOMAN ABROAD

THE SELECTED LANTERN SLIDES OF MARY T.S. SCHÄFFER

*The Rockies,
Japan & Taiwan*

by MICHALE LANG

RMB
Victoria Vancouver Calgary

I think in every woman's heart (perhaps man's too) is a desire longing for even a small spot to call "home".

It's been eight years since I felt I could afford one & do all [illegible] things I want to do, [illegible] now being certain [illegible] it now.

A [illegible] said "Why doesn't she [illegible] shack at Banff?" [illegible] her, was like [illegible] which really [illegible] the story. Mary Jo's remark has hung in my brain a long time. Was there a possibility of having a home? The way has opened for me to use a small cottage here for a couple of months

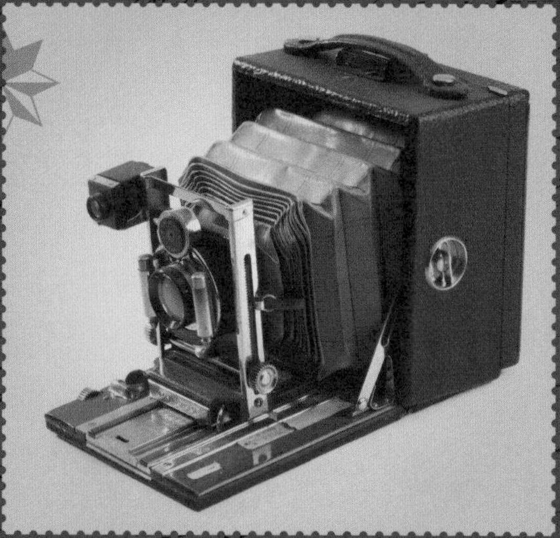

For all of the adventurous women I have known.
And for only one man, Richard Lang.

Rocky Mountain Books
www.rmbooks.com

Library and Archives Canada Cataloguing in Publication

Lang, Michale, 1956-
An adventurous woman abroad : the lantern slides of Mary T.S. Schäffer / written and compiled by Michale Lang ; photographs by Mary T.S. Schäffer.

(The Whyte Museum of the Canadian Rockies presents)
Includes bibliographical references and index.
ISBN 978-1-926855-21-9

1. Schäffer, Mary T.S. (Mary Townsend Sharples), 1861–1939—Travel. 2. Women travelers—Rocky Mountains, Canadian (B.C. and Alberta). 3. Women travelers—Japan. 4. Women travelers—Taiwan. 5. Rocky Mountains, Canadian (B.C. and Alta.)—Description and travel. 6. Japan—Description and travel. 7. Taiwan—Description and travel. I. Schäffer, Mary T.S. (Mary Townsend Sharples), 1861–1939 II. Title. III. Series: Whyte Museum of the Canadian Rockies presents

FC219.S324 2011   917.123'32042   C2011-900275-2

Printed in China

Rocky Mountain Books acknowledges the financial support for its publishing program from the Government of Canada through the Canada Book Fund (CBF) and the province of British Columbia through the British Columbia Arts Council and the Book Publishing Tax Credit.

Canadian Heritage Patrimoine canadien

BRITISH COLUMBIA ARTS COUNCIL
Supported by the Province of British Columbia

This book was produced using FSC®-certified, acid-free paper, processed chlorine free and printed with soya-based inks.

FSC
www.fsc.org

MIX
Paper from
responsible sources
FSC® C016973

Contents

Acknowledgements

Books are never the work of only the author. I have many people to thank for their support and patience. I thank my husband, who has supported me and been infinitely patient about all the hours I cannot spend with him because I am writing or because he is reading my work to give me feedback. My mother is proud of everything I do, no matter what, and her pride in my modest accomplishments always makes me want to do better.

Ted Hart, who has been my mentor and supporter since I began working at the Whyte Museum, has my immense gratitude. He volunteers to make sure I do not blunder into some morass of historic inaccuracy. Elizabeth Kundert-Cameron keeps me humble in the nicest possible way. And I thank Don Bourdon for providing additional information about Mary's lantern slides. Lena Goon never misses my sometimes thoughtless errors. I would also like to extend my thanks to Meaghan Smith, who assisted me in researching this book and kept me laughing with her quirky sense of humour. All of these people kept me honest and for this I am deeply grateful.

Beki Hunt and her partner Amour Lee have read the information about the Amis people and have been of great assistance in making sure it was correct. I am in their debt. Beki, I am so happy we drifted together on a canal in Southern France.

The Alberta Historical Resources Foundation provided funding for my research and this made it possible for me to escape to my writing retreat to review and process the wonderful research materials that I had gathered from the Whyte Museum's archives and other sources. I thank them for making this possible. I would also like to thank the Archives Society of Alberta, which provided funding for the digitization of Mary's lantern slides, making them more accessible to myself as well as other researchers. The Whyte Museum of the Canadian Rockies Board of Directors continually provides its support and encouragement. They understand the importance of research to museums in a way that few other boards I have encountered seem able to grasp. It is a privilege to work with them as they continue to guide the direction of this wonderful organization.

I would also like to thank Don Gorman, the publisher of Rocky Mountain Books, for his faith in me, his deep interest in the Whyte Museum's collections and for his support through a difficult time last year as my first book in the series was about to be submitted. As I continue to spout ideas for yet more books in the series, his enthusiasm is a wonderful encouragement. I would also like to thank Don for assigning excellent editors and proofreaders to my work and for producing high-quality books that look beautiful. Speaking of which, thanks also must go to Chyla Cardinal, who is a highly talented designer. I especially thank you, Chyla, for your choice of fonts, which any designer will tell you are fundamental to both a book's beauty and readability. For the amazing images, I have to thank D.L. Cameron, who is a scanning genius. My thanks also go to remarkable photographers Craig Richards of the Whyte Museum and Owen Melenka of the Glenbow Museum.

Finally, I thank Mary Schäffer for living her life so fully and for leaving such remarkable records of her time on this earth, where she walked gently and with an abiding sense of wonder. She is an inspiration to me and I only wish I could have met her in the backcountry. Her story is one that deserves to be told again and again.

MARY AND ME

*No-one may know I went among those hills with a broken heart
and only on the high places could I learn that I and mine were
very close together. We dare not tell those beautiful thoughts,
they like to say "explorer" of me, no, only a hunter of peace.*
—Mary Warren [1928][1]

When I hike the trails that Mary Schäffer's hobnail boots trod 100 years ago, I feel a kinship to this famous Victorian woman adventurer of the Canadian Rockies. I consider what I might have in common with her. Perhaps most important, Mary came to the Canadian Rockies as a "hunter of peace."[2] I too come to these mountains seeking peace. I share her love of the mountains, of alpine meadows, clear glacial lakes, wildflowers and wild creatures. Banff has become my home as it was hers. Like her, I am interested in photography and art, although I share her talent for neither. Mary's deep interest in indigenous people and history is the other common ground we walk. Mary was an extraordinary woman for her time, but she is someone I can easily relate to.

I first connected with Mary through her writing. Although she was widely published, she referred to her writing with humility, noting, "I am only a story teller."[3] Many books have told the stories of Mary Schäffer's adventures in the Canadian Rockies, including her own *Old Indian Trails of the Canadian Rockies* (1911), as well as *A Hunter of Peace: Mary T.S. Schäffer's Old Indian Trails of the Canadian Rockies* (1980) and *No Ordinary Woman: the Story of Mary Schäffer Warren* (2001). This book takes a new look at those adventures through Schäffer's lantern slides and the scripts she wrote to present them. It also tells the story of her travels to Asia, which has only been summarized in previous publications.

While conducting research in the Whyte Museum archives, I was struck particularly by two scripts that Mary wrote for lantern slide presentations. In the early 1900s, lantern slide presentations were similar to today's digital productions like PowerPoint. In fact, lantern slides were so popular during Victorian times that they became nearly as common as television is today. The two scripts have been included here and are entitled "In the Heart of the Canadian Rockies, Part I"

and "In the Heart of the Canadian Rockies, Part II: At the Head Waters of the Saskatchewan and Athabaska: A Sequel to 'In the Heart of the Canadian Rockies.'" Mary prepared them for First World War soldiers convalescing in British hospitals and they effectively summarize her backcountry travels. Despite the fragility of the glass upon which they are mounted, the vast majority of the lantern slides that she used in her presentations have survived. The slides are now in the Whyte Museum archives and they have been reunited with the scripts to make up the core of this book. They project Mary's view of the Rockies, with her hand-coloured lantern slides illustrating her words.

In addition to these two scripts, two of her articles also stood out: "A Glimpse of the Headhunters of Formosa," which was never published, and a previously published article, "With the Hairy Ainus." These two articles and the photographs that accompany them tell the colourful story of Mary's travels to Asia. I have included them to provide a more balanced picture of this remarkable woman beyond her adventures in the Canadian Rockies. These articles particularly demonstrate her deep interest in indigenous people and her determination to travel untrammelled trails to come into contact with them.

It is easy to forget that women in Canada were only granted the right to vote in federal elections in 1918, less than 100 years ago. Despite the restrictions upon women of her time, before they even had the vote, Mary Schäffer was exploring the backcountry of the Canadian Rockies to find a lake that had been seen only by indigenous people and a very few white men before her.[4] As if that were not enough, in 1911, at the request of the Canadian government, Mary also surveyed that lake (Maligne Lake), an undertaking that was regarded as the exclusive domain of men in the early 20th century. Surveyor and Alpine Club of Canada President Arthur O. Wheeler conducted a survey of Maligne Lake later in 1911 and was furious to discover that Mary had already done so.

As a Quaker woman, Mary had more freedom than many other Victorian women. Adherents of her faith believed in the equality of men and women, but this belief did not extend to the rest of early-20th-century society. Although Mary had a modicum of freedom more than other women, she was still very much a woman of her time. She held views we would now consider imperialist. She used language, particularly in relation to indigenous people, that today we may find offensive. But this does not diminish her accomplishments or make her less admirable.

Because of her humour, humility and pragmatism, we can appreciate Mary's accomplishments even more. In a most humble manner, she simply took both accomplishments and impediments in stride. Mary consistently emphasized that her own exploits were not exceptional; that "with reasonable care, caution and good animals, one may travel almost anywhere in that great wilderness with perfect safety."[5] She assured her readers that wilderness travel involves "no lasting hardships, only life, great broad, inspiriting life."[6]

Despite her encouraging words to others, Mary did not start out as an adventurer. When she first came to the Rockies as a new bride in 1889, she was a reluctant explorer who stayed close to the railway tracks that had carried her here. She thought of herself as "a delicate girl, not staunch enough to attempt some of 'the first climbs' of which [she] was hearing daily or to penetrate some of the 'new' valleys of which others spoke."[7] Her first foray away from the tracks came in 1893 when renowned Banff guide and outfitter Tom Wilson took Mary and her first husband Charles Schäffer camping on the shores of Lake Louise. They travelled the first 40 miles to Laggan Station, now Lake Louise, on top of a boxcar. For the entire trip, they were showered in soot from the steam engine. Then, with great trepidation, they climbed on horses to finish the journey to the lake. Upon their arrival, she described the lakeshore as "a dismal, stump-filled swamp, a breeding place for myriads of mosquitoes."[8] She looked out the next morning "upon that magnificent scene with chattering teeth and shivering bodies, and vowed never again to camp in the Canadian Rockies."[9] It took time for her to overcome her reservations and venture farther afield.

Although she developed a passion for travel in high places, Mary was not a true mountaineer. She realized this when she decided to climb Mount Wilcox. In Part I of her slideshow, Mary described her terrifying experience. Mount Wilcox (Wilcox Peak) is located in Jasper National Park in the upper Sunwapta River Valley opposite Mount Kitchener. It is 2884 m (9,462 ft.) in height and was named by J. Norman Collie after Walter D. Wilcox, an American student from Yale University who participated in some of the earliest explorations in the Canadian Rockies.[10]

Although Mary enjoyed "the magnificent views, the purity of the snows, the wonderful silence, the glissades when the hardest work is over,"[11] her description of climbing Mount Wilcox makes it clear she did not enjoy climbing. It was not something she was willing to try again. She remarked, "Why do something with your heart in your mouth all the time?" Mary much preferred riding to climbing. "Ride? I would go with an Indian pony any place, swim, jump, or follow my beloved Nibs when I was snow-blind, over Cataract Pass, but preserve me from climbing."[12] Mary may not have appreciated climbing, but she had a deep interest in stories of climbing and exploring by those who had come before her. I share these sentiments.

Mary read every account she could find about exploring the Canadian Rockies. Throughout her early travels, Mary had eagerly conversed with hunters, trappers, adventurers and explorers. From one of these, Jimmy Simpson, she heard about a lake to the north that the Stoney Nakoda called

"*Chaba Imne*, now Maligne Lake." Mary's interest in "old Indian trails" eventually led her to that lake, following a rudimentary map she obtained from her Nakoda friend Sampson Beaver.

Mary's friendship with Sampson was no accident, as she had developed an interest in Aboriginal people from an early age. It began when she overheard stories from a visiting relative, "Cousin Jim," who had fought in the American Indian Wars in the mid-19th century. Cousin Jim regaled her parents with horrific tales of the Wild West. Akin to children today sneaking a peek at late-night television, Mary would creep out of her bed to listen to the gruesome stories her parents considered unsuitable for children. "With premeditated daring and quiet defiance the child [Mary] slipped out to the veranda clutching her own special small stool which she deposited in an obscure, vine-clad, darkened corner, and there waited with what courage she could the coming of this unknown here who was having a 'grown-up' dinner with her parents."[13] Throughout her life, Mary would pursue things that were considered unsuitable by many of her peers, but as an adult she did not hide her rebellion.

I live in a time when it is much easier for women to do things that during Mary's time were the sole domain of men. Backcountry travel has become acceptable for women and easier for men and women alike. She and her travelling companion Mary (Mollie) Adams would spend the winters planning their summer trips. Mollie was a geology teacher at Columbia College. She and Mary met through their mutual interest in flowers. In 1905 Mary and Mollie travelled with other women in their party, but they soon discovered that they most enjoyed one another's company and that two was the perfect number for the trail.

In Mary's time, it took a pack train of ten or more horses to explore the Canadian Rockies for the summer. A weighty canvas tent would provide the roof over her head while on the trail but it was not always a waterproof shelter. When she tried a new lighter-weight tent made of Egyptian sail-cloth, she discovered to her dismay that it had a tendency to catch fire. Neither was her bedding entirely comfortable. On her 1908 trip Mary noticed that "[a] most peculiar odour clung to the blankets of my bed. A neatly conducted conversation brought out the fact that those blankets and some raw bear-skins had spent considerable time in each other's society during the spring."[14] Only after two washings in a hand basin did they smell fresh again. Her accommodation and bedding were a far cry from our high-tech equipment today.

Nowadays we can buy every description of lightweight dried foods that make days or weeks in the backcountry tolerable, but this was not the case in Mary's day. While she and Mollie experienced some success in testing new food for their backcountry travels, a few of their experiments were complete failures. In the spring of 1908

Mary spent hours preparing eight pounds of pinole, a type of cornmeal, only to find that "it had a taste which hung on for hours, its consistency was that of a mouthful of sand, and its grittiness was all over you, inside and out."[15] Eventually, after even the horses refused to eat it, Mary noted, "It may be all right if you are starving, but in times of peace and plenty, beware." They could sometimes supplement their diet with fresh meat in the form of wild game, but even that was not always palatable. Mary told a funny story about a goat so tough that "though 'K' [Sid Unwin, another of their guides] pounded his steaks to jelly on the stones, and boiled and simmered his legs for hours, he failed to be 'chewable' let alone digestible."[16]

Clothing was another issue. We now have quick-dry, washable clothing for activities such as riding and hiking. Rainproof gear is readily available. When Mary was visiting the Rockies, women were expected to wear skirts and behave in a refined manner befitting a Victorian lady. This was at a time when the local newspaper, the *Banff Crag and Canyon,* ran an article expounding that "pants are made for men and not women. Women are made for men and not for pants."[17] This simply echoed the dress codes of the time, and although Quaker women such as Mary were expected to dress in less colourful clothing than other Victorian women, they were still bound by these codes, both written and unwritten.[18] But as soon as she was out of sight of "civilized" onlookers, Mary had no qualms about donning breeches and burying her skirt in a pack for the rest of her travels in the short Rocky Mountain summer. Although she sometimes felt compelled to dig out her skirt when they were visiting the few trappers they encountered along the way, she relished her practical buckskin and breeches to protect her from the weather on the trail.

Mary once wrote, "No one need ever think he is going to avoid the weather; no mountains were

16

[Boots worn out from a summer on the trail, 1908].[19]

ever made without it, least of all the Rockies."[20] On a sunny summer day, there is no place more beautiful than the Canadian Rockies, but one is as likely to encounter snow as sun. Neither is travel in the backcountry of the Canadian Rockies without risk. Mary recounted wild river crossings and runaway horses. Pests of all sorts, particularly mosquitoes, were ubiquitous, and in those days there were no effective repellents. "How we sopped our faces with citronella till we hated the name, and applied a highly advertised mosquito 'dope' which was grey and greasy, and whose only virtue as a destroyer seemed to be to catch the enemy by the wings and leave him kicking and struggling on the very spot which we wished to preserve from his ravages."[21] The larger pests were the rats that were the bane of Mary's travels from the Canadian Rockies to Formosa (now Taiwan). In whatever land Mary and her companions travelled, rats would jump uninvited into their beds or keep them awake with their nightly skitters.

Despite all of the hardships along the way, Mary loved to travel and she followed her interests around the world. She was always interested in collecting botanical specimens or learning about the history of the places she visited. But foremost, from the Canadian Rockies to Japan to Formosa, she pursued her deep passion to see the indigenous people who she strongly believed were disappearing entirely from the face of the earth. And in some ways she was right. In Formosa some of

the tribes that were still living during Mary's time no longer exist.

How did I learn this? In the summer of 2010, 102 years after Mary's 1908 trip to Formosa and Japan, I took a vacation in France. While travelling in the Agens area, I met a young Canadian woman named Beki Hunt who spends her summers working on a barge in France and her winters teaching English in Taiwan. She happened to mention that her life partner, Amour Lee, is from one of the indigenous tribes of Taiwan, the Amis. I asked in astonishment, "You mean he's one of the headhunters of Formosa?" During her ten summers working in France, she said she had never met anyone with any knowledge of the indigenous people of Taiwan, let alone the fact that some of them had been headhunters. I then explained to Beki that I had chanced upon my rudimentary knowledge because I was working on a book about Mary Schäffer, an early-20th-century woman who had gone seeking the indigenous people of

Formosa in the winter of 1908. Fortunately, I had brought copies of Mary's lantern slide images and the article she had written about her journey. This bit of serendipity led to the great delight of engaging with someone who could answer my questions about the "headhunters of Formosa." I am amazed when things like this happen. It gives me shivers every time I think about it. Mary's travels were often punctuated by serendipity as well. Her chance meetings with people along the trail resulted in some of her most remarkable photographs and stories. Mary's pursuit to learn more about indigenous people inevitably took her off the beaten path to greater adventures.

As a girl, Mary could never have anticipated the adventures that lay ahead. She had come a long way from her first timid forays into the Canadian Rockies and she had become a seasoned, audacious traveller. The interests that led her around the world may have sprouted during her childhood rambles through the Pennsylvania countryside with her amateur naturalist father, with Cousin Jim's stories playing in the back of her head, but they grew with each trip to the Rockies.

MARY'S INFLUENCES

Quaker Roots

I always blamed it on a wonderful grandmother ... She spoke
in Meeting like one inspired ... if I ever dared to get up in
church it would be no peaceful place for some folk.
—Mary Warren [1933?] [22]

Mary Sharpless[23] (Schäffer) was born on October 4, 1861, to Alfred and Elizabeth Sharpless in West Chester, Pennsylvania. Her two younger brothers, Frederick and Herman, were born in 1866 and 1871, respectively. As was not uncommon at the time, an older brother Henry, born in 1858, died several months before Mary's birth. Another brother, named Joseph, born 1859, died in 1869.

During Mary's childhood, her father would take her out into the Chester County countryside and teach her about flowers and rocks and other natural wonders. This early-acquired basis in natural history undoubtedly sparked her later interest in

Mary Schäffer in Quaker costume

the flora and fauna of the Canadian Rockies. Her interest in botany persisted throughout her life and led her to explore many areas she would not otherwise have visited.

One of the reasons Mary had a rather unusual freedom for a woman of her time was her Quaker heritage. As a Quaker woman, Mary received a good education. She was also included in activities such as family vacations to remote places like the American West. This coincided with Briton Thomas Cook spearheading tourism in the 1860s by offering working-class excursions to the country and seaside. Their popularity soon spread to the upper-middle and gentry classes, and then crossed the Atlantic to wealthy residents of the northeastern United States. Mary's family fit into the upper-middle-class category. Around 1876, only four years after the establishment of Yellowstone, the first national park in the United States, Mary's railroad travels began. At the age of 14, she journeyed with her family across the Great Plains to

California. This first trip west was Mary's first introduction to indigenous people beyond the stories she had overheard from Cousin Jim.

Although Mary enjoyed her early travels, she was limited by health problems. Throughout her life, she suffered from neuralgia, a persistent and painful physical condition, but she did not let ill health stop her from pursuing a full life. In 1889 Mary married physician and amateur natural historian Dr. Charles Schäffer of Philadelphia and moved to his city home. Charles was 24 years her senior.

Mary Schäffer, January 22, 1902

VAUX FAMILY FONDS (V653/NG 4 – 959)

A Reluctant Explorer

I was at that time an American citizen
absolutely enthralled with any data
I could obtain of those who had gone
before in the most beautiful land of
the world – the Canadian Rockies.
—Mary Schäffer, 1903[24]

In 1871 Prime Minister Sir John A. Macdonald had promised a railway to link the new country of Canada from coast to coast. The government found the new route expensive to build, particularly when it hit the barrier of the Canadian Rocky Mountain range, with its steep passes, rock slides and avalanches. Although the railway was seen as a means of ultimately settling the West and thereby recovering the cost of its construction, tourism was seen as a means to begin paying the bills as soon as possible. In large part thanks to William Cornelius Van Horne, Canadian Pacific Railway's (CPR's) bigger-than-life general manager during construction through the mountains, the transcontinental railway was completed in 1885. And to help pay for the new line, Van Horne was determined to bring tourists to the Canadian Rockies. "If we can't export the scenery, we'll import the tourists," he said.[25] It is little wonder that Mary Schäffer refers to Van Horne as that "famous man" in one of her commentaries.

Rest stops along the CPR line were established to provide travellers with food and lodging before sleeping and dining cars were added to trains. Rest stops such as Mount Stephen House in Field, BC, and Glacier House near Rogers Pass, BC, opened in 1887. The popularity of these rest stops quickly led to the development of luxury accommodation throughout the mountains. By 1889 the CPR had hired 12 travelling passenger agents to attract tourist traffic to the Canadian West with vivid descriptions of the splendour of the Rockies. Before long the railway was offering the services of outfitters, such as Tom Wilson, as well as Swiss guides at their mountain resorts. The days of recreational tourism in the Rockies had begun.

Mary Schäffer's watercolour paint-box, circa early 1900s

Mary and Charles Schäffer were among the tourists lured by CPR's advertisements. Mary first saw the Canadian Rockies with her new husband when, following his attendance at the 1889 Canadian Medical Convention in Toronto, they accompanied the convention on an excursion to the Rockies. This first trip came only four years after the 1885 completion of CPR's transcontinental line and the establishment of the Banff Hot Springs Reserve, the precursor to Banff National Park. The year 1885 also marked the appearance of rolled film, replacing glass plates and making photography much more accessible to amateurs, especially travellers. Charles had plans to author a botanical book on the wildflowers of the Canadian West. Each of these events would have an impact on Mary's interests.

Mary and Charles were impressed enough on their first visit to the Rockies

(SCM.05.19)

to return two years later – and every summer thereafter. Throughout the 1890s they visited often, collecting botanical specimens, and Mary soon perfected the art of botanical illustration under her husband's watchful eye.

Left: Alpine Flower, Mary Schäffer, watercolour on paper, 1891

Below: Mary Schäffer's ceramic watercolour paintbox, circa early 1900s

In 1885 Mary was an elite, pampered, well-educated traveller who wanted to see the sights from the relative comfort of a railway carriage. Although she and Charles took short, guided excursions into the mountains, they liked to return to the comfortable overnight accommodation offered at the new mountain hotels. Like most travellers today, Mary did not stray far from the means of access that brought her there. Although it was a photo of Lake Louise that had first attracted her to the Canadian Rockies, Mary's first camping experience there in 1893 left her less than impressed.

In 1898 the Schäffers participated in a Philadelphia Photographic Society expedition to Emerald Lake in the Banff reserve. At the Big Bend of the Columbia River,[26] the couple took their first foray beyond the reach of the train whistle. Mary also grew increasingly adventurous on her day trips with the Vauxes, another Quaker family from Philadelphia who travelled extensively in the Canadian Rockies. Although she may not have begun truly exploring the backcountry, these were her first steps toward her later adventures. Throughout this time, Mary took an active interest in stories of indigenous people and exploration.

Mary's Interest in Indigenous Peoples

Cousin Jim was a bit of the far west himself, he belonged to Uncle Sam's army which was steadily pushing the many tribes back from the advancing white settlers. The small eavesdropper had been told Indian tales and had a ghostly idea of what they were and how they lived, about as ghostly as most folk still have who live always behind the vines on dark verandas and in small villages.
—Mary Schäffer[27]

Mary was first exposed to stories of the Wild West and indigenous people by a relative, 'Cousin

Jim', when she was only four years old. Mary's parents were upset when they caught her eavesdropping on adult conversations of Cousin Jim's experiences in the Indian Wars. They sent her to bed immediately, but the stories left a deep impression. One story that particularly stayed with her involved the "destruction of an Indian village that had been so complete even the women and children had been killed. Examining the carnage, he had made a heart-rending discovery, a live baby peeping out from under the shelter of its mother's dead body. Hearing this was too much for Mary and she let out a sob that led to her discovery and subsequent banishment to her bedroom never to hear the poor babe's fate."[28]

Mary's parents may have been even more upset with her than they were if they had realized how deeply she would be affected by her childhood eavesdropping on Cousin Jim's stories about indigenous people. Mary later wrote: "The baby face, the dead mother, the smoking tepees remained in a child's mind forever after and governed many an act as she grew older. She never spoke of what she heard that night, but the shadows of the story always hung on her horizon"[29] It is little wonder, then, that she carried a pistol along the first time she boarded a train bound for the western United States.

Because indigenous peoples had fascinated Mary since childhood, meeting them had always been a highlight of her travels. Though her first trip to the Rockies was conditioned by societal prejudices and the intense fear of indigenous people that permeated colonial society in the aftermath of the North-West Rebellion of 1885, she quickly realized she had nothing to fear. In Part I of her Canadian Rockies lantern-slide show, she remarks, "Many years ago we were driving to the lake [Minnewanka] when we suddenly beheld quite a party of Indians coming our way. The writer was utterly 'green.' Frightened of the savages (?) and when the driver said 'jump' she was out of that rig before the word was right out. The Indians took in the situation, politely dropped down into the gully, grunted 'how,' laughed and the incident was closed. But never again had the Indians any terror for the easterner, the smiles made us friends, a friendship which continues to this day."[30]

Mary had a much friendlier attitude toward First Nations people than did many of her contemporaries. She likely had little idea of the impact that white settlement would ultimately have on her friends. Treaty Number 7, signed in 1877,[31] changed the lives of the Stoney Nakoda people forever. Upon the signing of the treaty, they surrendered traditional territory for settlement by non-indigenous people, and their hunting was restricted to the areas of land reserved for them. The First Nations people Mary encountered during her mountain travels of 1907 and 1908, such as the Sampson Beaver family, still held onto their traditional lives, hunting and trading throughout the area. Her meetings with them gave her a hint of

what their lives might have been like before white settlement began to encroach.

Mary Schäffer's buckskin jacket, Stoney First Nations, circa early 1900s

*In his quiet fashion he told in simple
language of the morning which had been set
apart for his branch of the army to destroy
a village of hostile Indians … the usual
plan for obliterating such a nuisance was
to wipe out the village – it was the only
way understood in those days (the 1860s).*
—*Mary Schäffer*[32]

Mary's writing reflects the views of her time. During her lifetime, First Nations people were most commonly known as "Indians." Although "Indians" is still used today, even in government policy, most indigenous people in Canada prefer to be called First Nations. In Mary's time, the vast majority of non-Natives referred to indigenous people as "savages." In the Victorian era, First Nations women were called "squaws." Today, we would consider this a racial slur with sexual implications, but Mary even refers to herself and her travelling companion Mollie as "white squaws" in her later writings. Mary refers sentimentally to the sweet or musical voices of the Aboriginal women she met, both in Canada and in Asia, and how they greeted her photographic sessions "with musical laughter and little giggles."[33] Today, we might cringe at the terms that reflect her imperialistic attitudes, but in Mary's time, these terms were in common use and her attitudes were much more sympathetic than many of her contemporaries. For example, she wrote of herself: "This was Mary's fever, an all-consuming one, a new-born love for a race that even her young mind taught her had not had fair treatment from the interlopers of their land,"[34] and "it was the theory that they were just human like herself with warm affections if only her [Mary's] own people would take the trouble to study them."[35] Because Mary's views offer a sympathetic barometer of her times, I have left the terms we now consider discriminatory where they originally appeared in her text.

Despite her willingness to take on new adventures, Mary sometimes voiced concerns about social transgressions when she and her companions occasionally encountered other travellers. L.Q. Coleman (brother of famed explorer Dr. A.P. Coleman) masked his surprise at finding ladies travelling so far from the railway. But when Mary and Mollie encountered butterfly collector Mary de la Beach Nichol still looking "every inch a lady,"[36] Mary feared that "with no hat, clad in a boy's dark blue shirt, a scarlet kerchief at the neck, an old Indian beaded coat on, there was little of Philadelphia left clinging to [her own] shoulders."[37] Nonetheless her practicality led her to abandon her skirt and sidesaddle as soon as "the village and critics were well left behind, [she] poked the old thing into [her] duffel bag and that was the end of anything but the modern breeches, till [we] hailed back to civilization."[38] Rudyard Kipling's account of his encounter with Mary and Mollie provides an interesting observation:

As we drove along the narrow hill-road a piebald pack-pony with a china-blue eye came round a bend, followed by two women, black-haired, bareheaded, wearing beadwork squaw-jackets and riding straddle. A string of pack-ponies trotted through the pines behind them.

"Indians on the move?" said I. "How characteristic!"

As the women jolted by, one of them very slightly turned her eyes, and they were, past any doubt, the comprehending equal eyes of the civilised white woman which moved in that berry-brown face.[39]

When Kipling later met Mary dressed in an elegant evening gown at Mount Stephen House in Field, BC, he had difficulty believing she was the same person he had encountered on the trail. Mary was making history with her unorthodox behaviour. Others would follow in her footsteps as she trod those of earlier adventurers.

FOLLOWING THEIR FOOTSTEPS

Very few men, save trappers, had gone far to the north, and no women had felt that they had any particular business that way.
—*Mary Schäffer, c1914–1918*[40]

From her first trip to the Canadian Rockies, Mary had been interested in the history of the area, but her interest became increasingly pragmatic. When she began travelling in the backcountry with Mollie Adams, she wanted to learn more about the routes followed by those who came before her. She and Mollie would spend their winters preparing for their travels of the coming summer, devouring every book and article they could find, from the journals of Father De Smet and Reverend Rundle, to Palliser's expedition report, to Jean Habel's, James Outram's and A.P. Coleman's accounts. Mary and Mollie listened to their stories of valleys of great beauty, of high unknown peaks, of little-known rivers, of un-named lakes, lying to the north and north-west of the country we knew so well, – "a fairyland, yet a land girt about with hardships, a land whose highway was a difficult trail or no trail at all. We fretted for the strength of man, for the way was long and hard, and only the tried and stalwart might venture where cold and heat, starvation and privation stalked ever at the explorer's heels. In meek despair we bowed our heads to the inevitable, to the cutting knowledge of the superiority of the endurance of man and the years slipped by.*[41]*

It is difficult for us to imagine what they faced, especially as women. The distance we travel now in less than a day took a whole summer in Mary's time. There were no reliable maps, no Global Positioning System (GPS) and only rough trails, often through muskeg or littered with deadfall. If you made a mistake, there were neither cell phones nor helicopter rescues. A good mount and a guide were an absolute necessity. This was truly a wilderness. But despite these challenges, Mary and Mollie increasingly drew inspiration from the accounts they read.

Missionary Explorers

Mary makes reference to Mount Rundle in Part I of her Canadian Rockies lantern-slide show: "This mountain received its name from the Rev. Dr. Rundle who as far back as 1840 had left his placid home in England to work among the Indians."[42] She is mistaken in how the mountain got its name. Mount Rundle was actually named by John Palliser in 1858 after the same Reverend Rundle to whom Mary is referring. Palliser was impressed that the Blackfoot in the area still showed signs of Rundle's influence despite the missionary's absence of over a decade.

Robert Terrill Rundle, born in 1811, was a missionary who visited the Banff area in the 1840s. During the years he spent doing missionary work among the Cree and Assiniboine, Rundle became very involved in their culture. He learned to speak Cree and even wrote hymns in the language.[43] Reverend Rundle kept a detailed journal of his missionary experience in Canada between 1840 and 1848, which has served as a valuable tool for historians. Rundle's journal is one of the first written accounts of a non-fur-trade employee's life in Alberta. The mountain after which he is named is located in the Bow River Valley, between the towns of Banff and Canmore, Alberta, on the boundary between Kananaskis and Banff parks. Its elevation is 2949 m (9,675 ft.). The mountain was first climbed in 1888 by James J. McArthur during his survey of the Bow Valley area.

Mary also refers to Father De Smet in her lantern slide script. Father Pierre-Jean De Smet, born in 1801, travelled through much of the Canadian Rockies in 1845 and 1846, documenting his journeys along the way. When De Smet was Superior of the Oregon Missions, he visited and established Catholic missions among the Native American tribes of what is today the northwestern corner of the United States and British Columbia.[44] De Smet had spent several years working with the Kootenay in the Oregon Territory missions with his church prior to 1845. He was then instructed to try to extend his work over the mountains with the Blackfoot tribe of the Plains. He crossed the eastern side of the mountains from the headwaters of the Columbia through the area of the Cross and Mitchell river systems, all in an effort to spread the Catholic gospel. In her lantern-slide show, Mary makes reference to "White Man's Pass."

White Man Pass is located in Banff National Park, adjacent to White Man Mountain and Red Man Mountain. John Palliser named the pass in 1858. Peakfinder[45] suggests "the "white man" for whom White Man Pass was named was Father De Smet, who camped on the pass in 1845. Mount Rundle and White Man Pass are just two of the many geographical features named by members of the Palliser Expedition.

The Palliser Expedition

Mary took great interest in the Palliser Expedition (1857–59), "which was the first "systematically scientific" exploration of the western interior region of Canada. As a result of its favourable observations regarding the agricultural potential of the territory, the British government decided to proceed with colonization plans in order to discourage American dreams of 'manifest destiny' in the Canadian West."[46]

Perhaps this particular interest of Mary's stemmed from her having met one of the members of the Palliser Expedition, Sir James Hector, during her visit to Glacier House in 1903. He was at an advanced age when Mary met him, but at the age of 23, shortly after finishing his medical training, he had served as geologist and naturalist on the Palliser Expedition. In an article entitled "Palliser's Expedition, Some Intimate Glimpses," Mary describes their meeting:

I was sitting quietly in the small rotunda of the little hotel, sketching I think, when my ears caught the remark: "I mean to see my grave!" Then came the profound thump of a fist on the counter of the office. One naturally takes an interest in any one who is on the hunt of his own grave and as I was always looking for anyone who had any history at his tongue's end, I slipped from my chair and quietly went to the desk to see if I could discover anything new. The charming hostess of many years' standing was listening to a rather under-sized and very emphatic man, rather stout who looked at least 70, though later I wondered if his work might not have aged him. Knowing my love of discovering historical people, she looked at him and at me and said: "Sir James may I introduce you to Mrs. Blank, who takes such an interest in this special western part of Canada?" I do not believe I gasped, but was profoundly astounded to discover I had come in touch with the famous doctor who had helped write Palliser's journal and who had done so much toward opening a part of the Rockies. I had not seen Palliser's book at that time, only heard scraps of it; so as politely as possible I asked where he meant to look for his grave. He seemed delighted to find someone who would take an interest in his boyhood travels and in a few moments I was a happy listener … They followed up the Kicking Horse River as now known, when they decided they saw better footing on the other side. "I completely forgot about the limber heels of my pony, so eager was I to get over with the rest of our party. The pony refused the wild stream and I gave him quite a good blow on the rump. That was the last I knew till I woke in time to behold a grave yawning for me. My friends had decided I was dead and they were doing the last respectful act – putting me under the sod. This I sternly refused and having recovered my wind was ready to go off again up that wild stream.[47]

In this article Mary also tells the sad tale that ended Hector's final visit to Canada. "In the afternoon of that day, Sir James was attending his son, who seemed to be suffering great pain. At last he called in my husband, who instantly diagnosed it as appendicitis and advised instant removal to hospital in Revelstoke." Eventually, Hector and his son were put on a train to Revelstoke and everyone at Glacier House waited to hear the outcome. "Toward night came the telegram: 'Twenty-four hours too late. We could not save him.'" Hector's son was buried in Canada and Hector returned to his home in New Zealand a broken man.

James Hector, and Edward Whymper, the first man to make the ascent of the Matterhorn, at Glacier House, 1903

MARY SCHÄFFER FONDS (V527/PS I – 283)

Dr. A.P. Coleman

In Part I of Mary's slide presentation, she mistakenly refers to Dr. A.P. Coleman as Dr. P.A. Coleman but it is clear that she had a great deal of respect for him. Dr. Arthur Philemon Coleman was born in 1852 in Lachute, Quebec, where his father was stationed as a Wesleyan minister. He was an excellent student and a gifted artist. He chose science over art as a career, however. He specialized in geology, having obtained his Ph.D. in Germany in 1881.[48]

Between 1884 and 1908 Coleman made eight trips of discovery to the Canadian Rockies. He reported on these in many journals and in his book *The Canadian Rockies: New and Old Trails* (1911). When Coleman visited the Rockies, he hired members of the Stoney and Iroquois tribes to help with cooking, packing, guiding and trail-blazing.

Coleman was a charter member of the Alpine Club of Canada.

Jean Habel and Sir James Outram

Mary also refers to both Jean Habel and Sir James Outram in Part II of her slide presentation. Jean Habel was another early explorer in the Rocky Mountains. Habel was a tall, dignified mathematics professor from Berlin. Highly regarded in mountaineering circles, he is generally given credit for being the first white man to see Takakkaw Falls and is also credited with being the first to reach the Yoho Glacier, on his 1887 expedition. There is some controversy surrounding this latter claim, however. He may have heard about the Yoho Valley from Tom Wilson, a well-known Banff guide and outfitter. Throughout his lifetime, Wilson was adamant that he was the first one to explore the Yoho Valley. Wilson wrote:

With two others I went up the North Fork as we called it, past the Great Falls, past Laughing Falls and round by Twin Falls in 1884. We were prospecting for minerals. In 1897 in order to get the CPR interested in this region, I got a German professor [Habel] to go in and take photos and write it up in the magazines. I gave him three men – Frank Wellman, Fred Stephens and Ralph Edwards – and seven head of horses, provisions, tents etc. all for $7.00 per day and it cost me $11.50 per day cash and then the damn German took all the credit![49]

Habel was a member of the German-Austrian Alpine Club, where he gained high regard in the mountaineering community for his considerable climbing and exploration in the Alps and the Andes. Habel first came to Canada in 1896. In 1901 he returned to the Canadian Rockies and journeyed as far north as present-day Jasper National Park, becoming the first to reach the headwaters of the Athabasca River and see the north face of Mount Columbia.[50] In 1898 he produced a pamphlet describing his explorations in that part of British Columbia.[51] This is likely the account that Mary read.

In Part II of her Canadian Rockies lantern-slide show, Mary also mentions Sir James Outram, who, guided by Christian Kaufmann, was the first to reach the top of Mount Columbia, in 1902. Outram described the view from the summit as "simply marvellous." He later wrote, "The vast extent of these mountain-tops is extremely striking, especially in such untrodden regions as the Canadian Rockies freely offer. The charm of the unknown is mingled with the pleasures of recognition."[52] Although in 1903 Mary had little desire to stray from the beaten path, she read these accounts of Rocky Mountain explorers with great interest. Her natural curiosity would eventually get the better of her.

FROM RELUCTANT EXPLORER TO ADVENTURER

1904 to 1908

It's nice to say "we," but it was Mr. Warren's long outlook and Sid's
determination, Mollie and I were like the tail to an active horse.
—Mary Warren, 1928 [53]

It was not until 1904, 15 years after her first visit to the Rockies, at the age of 43, that Mary began to explore areas that would take her increasingly further away from the comfort of her earlier trips. At a time when most women barely ventured beyond their drawing room door, doors began to open for Mary that would lead her to places she never thought she would have the strength to go.

After losing her mother, her father and her beloved husband over a six-month period in 1903, Mary may have felt she had little more to lose. For the first time in her life, at the age of 42, she was alone. After all of these losses, she further discovered that she was left in a difficult financial situation and it took her some time to sort out her affairs. Mary commented on this time in her life: "All this taught me such a bitter lesson, to count my pennies, to lean on no-one, and make the best of the crumbling fortunes." [54] Rather than be defeated by her losses, Mary became increasingly independent.

To honour her husband Charles's memory, Mary decided to return to the Canadian Rockies the following summer to complete his proposed botanical guide. She persuaded Stewardson Brown, the curator of the Herbarium of the Academy of Natural Science in Philadelphia, to co-author the work. To obtain the botanical specimens, she needed to venture farther into the wilderness. Contacting Tom Wilson, she requested a guide who would toughen her up for the longer excursions required to complete the research. Wilson introduced her to Billy Warren, an English veteran of the Boer War. Warren took charge of travel logistics, obtaining horses and supplies. He taught Mary how to ride and set up camp. He determined the routes and often went ahead to ensure they were passable. She nicknamed Billy "Chief." In many of her written works, Mary acknowledges the importance of having a competent guide. *Alpine Flora of the Canadian Rocky Mountains* was published in 1907.

For the summers of 1904 and 1905, Mary convinced three Philadelphia educators, Misses Farr, Day and James, to join her in the field. They spent their first summer around Moraine Lake and the Yoho Valley, with an overnight excursion into the Ptarmigan Valley that fall. The following year, 1906, they began by working around Glacier House, Banff and Field. In July Mary and her old friend Mary Vaux, who travelled annually with her family to the Canadian Rockies, had the honour of being the first women to tour the Nakimu Caves, only two years after they were discovered by prospector and hunter C.H. Deutschmann.

The Nakimu Caves lie between upper and lower Cougar Valley in the Selkirk Mountains, just west of Rogers Pass on the Trans-Canada Highway. Nakimu is one of the largest cave systems in Canada, with 5.9 kilometres of passages that have been explored and mapped to date. Deutschmann named the caves Nakimu – a Shuswap word meaning "grumbling spirits." The two Marys visited the caves three years before Deutschmann sold his claim to the federal government for five thousand dollars, at which time he was appointed guide and custodian of the caves, a position he held until 1918.

Mary's 1906 season also included three longer excursions into the backcountry. She had sought travelling companions who shared her passion for alpine flora. She had also decided that the best companions would be Eastern U.S. women who could afford to travel and who were not restricted by family commitments. The four educators she was able to find shared her interest in flora, but she soon discovered that not all of them were suited to the rigours of tent and trail. In 1906 they began with a trip from Field to the Kootenay Plains, and enjoyed the destination so much they returned in July along a different route. Three of Mary's fellow travellers grew eager to return to the comforts of civilization, but Mary insisted on staying out the scheduled two weeks. "O ye who think five women, no matter how excellent they be, can all be of one mind on the trail, take a tip from me. In three days from starting, the little woman [Mollie Adams] and I were occupying one tent while the other three had the second. I do not think one unkind word was uttered by any one of the five, but we had separated into oil and water."[55] "We arrived back in the land of bath-tubs in due course and we two friends made all sorts of plans for the future, but firmly decided to keep our numbers down to two. We never broke our rule after that."[56]

Mary and Mollie extended their exploration north and west before being turned back by wintry weather. At the end of August 1906, they retraced their steps along the Pipestone and Siffleur rivers to the Kootenay Plains, where Mary returned often during her travels. There, she had the opportunity to meet Nakoda people. That same year Mary and Mollie photographed Nakoda women and children during their visits, particularly Sampson Beaver's wife and their daughter Frances Louise.

A homemade doll given to young Frances Louise Beaver won Mary a lasting friendship with the Beaver family. Seeing Mary's passion for travelling in the mountains, the Nakoda named Mary *Yahe-Weha*, or Mountain Woman.

40

The Indian Madonna, 1907

By 1907 Mary and Mollie were ready to take on the challenge of travelling through unmapped country. They had read so many accounts of adventure in the Canadian Rockies that finally the two women reached

41

the limit of all endurance, – to sit with folded hands and listen calmly to the stories of the hills we so longed to see, the hills which had lured and beckoned us for years before this long list of men had ever set foot in the country. Our cups splashed over. Then we looked into each other's eyes and said: "Why not? We can starve as well as they; the muskeg will be no softer for us than for them; the ground will be no harder to sleep upon; the waters no deeper to swim, nor the bath colder if we fall in," – so – we planned a trip.[57]

In 1907 Mary and Mollie decided to spend four months on the trail with their guides Billy Warren and Sid Unwin. Mary had been captivated by veteran guide Jimmy Simpson's mention of a mysterious lake north of the Brazeau, so they set off to find it.

Sidney Unwin, circa 1905

SID UNWIN FONDS (V25/PA 1)

Mary Schäffer Warren and Billy Warren

MOORE FAMILY FONDS (V439/PS 6)

While visiting the Nakodas again in 1907, Mary and her party were joined at their evening campfire by Sampson Beaver and Silas Abraham. Mary asked the Nakoda men about the spot they knew as *Chaba Imne*, or Beaver Lake (now Maligne Lake). Learning Sampson had been there as a child, Mary asked him to draw a map and he obliged. It was too late in the season to go searching for *Chaba Imne*, but it gave Mary an excellent reason to return the following year.

Finding Maligne Lake

As soon as possible, in June of 1908, Mary and Mollie set out with their guides on a quest for *Chaba Imne*. Stewardson Brown and his guide Reggie Holmes accompanied them. Sid Unwin's dog, Mr. Muggins, was the party's mascot. They had difficulty finding the trail over Poboktan Pass and were not sure which way to turn when they encountered a junction. A.P. Coleman's 1892 trail to the pass was challenging, with "quick changes from burnt timber to rock-climbing, muskeg, quicksand, scree slopes and mud-slides."[59] Mary describes Poboktan Pass (which she spells "Pobokton") as a miserable route. Sampson Beaver's simple map was unclear, but they decided to take their chances on the northward route. They finally crossed Maligne Pass but still could not see the lake. Sid Unwin decided to climb until he spotted it. Eight and a half hours later he returned to inform the camp they were on the right path.

When the group reached the lake the following morning Mary was thrilled: "Lake Louise is a pearl, Lake Maligne is a whole string of pearls."[60]

Mr. Muggins, 1908

The men immediately set about building a raft to explore the lake. They dubbed it HMS *Chaba Imne*. Mary had reservations about the safety of the craft: "Personally my sensations towards large bodies of water are similar to those of a cat, and though I begged to rough it, it was not so much to do something uncomfortable as to keep from drowning on an overtaxed raft."[61] She overcame her fear, however, and climbed aboard with the rest of the party, including Mr. Muggins, the dog.

Our first camp was just within Sampson's Narrows, which in our ignorance we took for the head of the lake. On our second day's row, we found that beyond the Narrows lay the most wonderful views of the whole lake, though previous to that we had all thought nothing in all our thousands of miles of travel in the Canadian Rockies, could equal what we were passing through. The task of propelling the bulky raft those three days was one deserving of a Hercules, but the workers realized we had found a lake the like of which there is not duplication on the eastern watershed of the Canadian Rockies, and freely and cheerfully gave of their strength without a murmur.[62]

This 1908 trip resulted in the naming of mounts Unwin, Warren and Mary Vaux as well as Samson Peak. Mary and her travelling companions named these mountains as reference points during their

Mt.[64] *Unwin from Camp*
[Rafting on Maligne Lake, 1908]

travels, but in 1911, when Mary was sent to survey Maligne Lake by Dr. Dowling, he requested that she send a map including her names for these geological features to the Geographical Board of Canada. The Board accepted Mary's names and they remain the official names of these features today.[63]

After exploring the lake, the party decided to head west toward the Yellowhead Trail and Mount Robson. As they attempted to cross the outlet of Maligne Lake, they had a close call with the undertow and were forced to take a longer route down the Poboktan Valley. By the time they reached the Sunwapta, Brown and Holmes had had enough and they decided to return to civilization taking nine horses with them. The two women carried on with their guides toward the Yellowhead Trail, Mount Robson and Tête Jaune Cache. As they reached homesteader Lewis Swift's farm (at today's Palisades, east of Jasper, Alberta), Swift exclaimed, "Women in your party?… Well,

The Swift Family [Mrs. Lewis Swift and four children, 1908]

MARY SCHÄFFER FONDS (V527/PS I – 93)

well, whatever brought them here? Prospecting or timber cruising? No? Now, look here, I've been in this valley thirteen years and they're the first white women I've seen around these parts. Are you sure they aint [sic] prospecting?"[65]

Mary's meeting with Mrs. (Suzette) Swift, who was Métis, is touching: "Then Mrs. Swift (oh, we women are all alike!) unearthed a box from beneath her bed and showed us a half dozen gowns made by herself, most of them her bridal finery, and

as we looked on the carefully trea-
sured garments, I realised – be it
mansion or shack – there is sure to
be stowed away just such a precious
horde around which a woman's heart
must always cling."[66] Mrs. Swift also
did fancywork, so Mary and Mollie
spent the afternoon shopping (a
very girly kind of activity), buy-
ing beautifully tanned and embroi-
dered gloves, moccasins and coats
from this "lonely Athabaska woman,"[67] some of which are now in the
Whyte Museum's collection.[68]

Ida Swift [1908]

MOORE FAMILY FONDS (V527/PS – 56)

Mary's buckskin shirts, donated to the Whyte Museum in 2009 by Mary's great-nephew, Eric, the son of Paul Sharpless, who travelled with Mary to Maligne Lake in 1911, and a lantern slide of Mary wearing one of the shirts.

The party left the Swifts' place to head for their last goal, Mount Robson. Their travels up the Miette Valley took them "up over high rock-bluffs, then down into sticky muddy bottoms where willows grew rank above our heads."[69] Crossing the Yellowhead Pass, they reached the Fraser River and followed a ghost of a trail that led them on past Moose Lake toward Robson, which they finally spotted. "To our weary, sunburnt eyes she loomed refreshingly up from behind a hill, cold, icy clean-cut, in a sky unclouded and of intensest blue."[70] They continued on to Tête Jaune Cache, where the visit of two women at first astonished the rugged men of the quiet village. After being welcomed with food, drink and good conversation, they departed the following day for home, loaded with mail and messages. Pouring rain and falling trees marked their passage around Moose Lake. Mary sustained an injury to her leg that was painful for the next year. Undeterred, they continued on, bade goodbye to the Swift family and made their way back to Banff.

It is clear from Mary's lantern slide presentation that she was deeply impressed with Lewis Swift's independent lifestyle in this rugged area. It would be only a short time before the land around Swift's homestead would no longer be a wilderness. The Grand Trunk Pacific, the northern transcontinental railway that would facilitate Mary's next visit, was already under construction.

Winter in Asia, 1908

During the winter of 1908, Mary and Mollie Adams were part of a group of American women to visit Japan and Formosa (Taiwan). Mary travelled with Mollie, Miss Bippinorth and Miss McDonald as guests of the Japanese government. Mary's dear friend Mollie, however, did not return. Tragically, she contracted pneumonia on the boat trip from Formosa back to Japan and died.

Although Mary was interested in collecting botanical specimens and pursuing photography in Asia, her overriding interest was to visit the indigenous peoples of Japan and Formosa. She had studied whatever she could find about their habits and customs and she was determined to learn more. She was particularly interested in comparing the people she met with the Aboriginal people she had encountered in North America. In the articles she wrote following her travels, "With the Hairy Ainus" and "A Glimpse of the Headhunters of Formosa," she drew parallels between the plight of many indigenous groups in the world that were being pushed farther into the hills by encroaching industry and development.

These visits again took her off the beaten path, which meant that travel was often uncomfortable, but Mary was not deterred by rats or by the gawking of people who had never seen a white woman. Despite warnings of dire consequences by her hosts and guides, her wishes were fulfilled. She returned with stories and photographs of the Ainu of Japan and of the Amis and Atayal of Formosa.

Return to Chaba Imne: 1911

With the loss of her dear friend Mollie, Mary went into a sort of retirement. She continued to write and speak about her trips as she had since her 1906 travels to the Kootenay Plains. Her work appeared in *The Bulletin of the Geographical Society of Philadelphia*, *Canadian Alpine Journal*, *Rod and Gun in Canada* and *Travel and Exploration*, as well as a brochure, *Untrodden Paths in the Canadian Rockies*, put out by Minneapolis, St. Paul & Sault Ste. Marie Railway Company. She also shared her stories in person, delighting audiences across North America – and Japan – with lantern-slide shows featuring her own hand-tinted slides. In 1911 she published tales of her 1907 and 1908 expeditions in *Old Indian Trails of the Canadian Rockies*.

In the same year, the Canadian Parliament passed the Dominion Forest Reserves and Parks Act. In order to better patrol the parks, their sizes were reduced. In June 1911 Jasper Park was reduced from 5,000 square miles (12,950 square kilometres) to a narrow strip bordering the Grand Trunk Pacific Railway, removing Maligne Lake from the park. Because of her writing and speaking success, Mary became a celebrity booster for the region, resulting in a surprising request for her to survey Maligne Lake, part of a campaign to keep the lake within Jasper Park. The request came from Dr. D.B. Dowling of the Geological Survey and Geographical Board. Mary responded with protests of incompetence. She had never surveyed anything! Eventually, she accepted instruction and equipment and, in May of 1911, set out once again for Maligne Lake.

The trip gave Mary the opportunity to experience "the difference between entering a country locked away from the world and the same one when the door was swinging wide open for the first time."[71] Her journey on the Grand Trunk Pacific included a stay in the boom town called Edmonton and rest stops at Edson and Hinton in Alberta. She made the journey from Edmonton on a colonist car transporting new immigrants to the Prairies – a far cry from the fine Canadian Pacific Railway cars to which she was accustomed.

Mary's party consisted of her sister-in-law Caroline Sharpless and her 11-year-old nephew Paul, as well as guides Jack Closson, Bruce Otto, Sid Unwin and one identified only as Wheeler. Paul had been suffering from whooping cough throughout the winter. Mary convinced Paul and his mother to accompany her, saying, "Give him

[Paul Sharpless and Sid Unwin?],
Looking up Pixie Valley [1911]

to me now and let me take him to a land where they have no coughs, where it is just ponies and fishing, bears and swimming, fresh air and fried bacon, and I'll guarantee to send him home to you with a stock of health and rosy cheeks which will last him all winter."[72]

Paul Sharpless with dead goat
at Maligne Lake, 1911

On this trip they approached the lake from the east. A crew had been hired to clear a trail for the survey expedition from the end of the rail line at Hinton to Maligne Lake, but when Mary's party reached its shores, new challenges began. The project was beset by errors and delays, partially due to Mary's inexperience at surveying. She struggled through an initial false start, and then she lost the surveying spool overboard the boat they were using. After nearly a month's wait for a new spool to be sent from Toronto, she began again, only to discover that her measurements were off. Realizing the metal in the tripod she was using was causing the inaccuracies, she was finally able to complete an accurate survey on July 23, one month after arriving at Maligne Lake.

Before Mary had even reached Hinton, Dowling was at her campsite, curious to know how the surveying had gone. He assured her that the small deviation she suspected in her measurements near the mouth of the Maligne was perfectly acceptable,

and encouraged her to send her measurements and map, including the names she had given various features around the lake, to the Geographical Board in Ottawa. When surveyor A.O. Wheeler claimed the names she selected, such as Mount Unwin and Mount Mary Vaux, were too personal and would inspire disrespect from the international community of geographers, his protests proved fruitless. With Dowling's support, Mary was able to ensure that her names were retained.

When Mary returned to Edmonton that August, she used her media appeal and carefully targeted comments to lobby for Maligne Lake's re-inclusion in Jasper Park. Responding to contemporary trends, she emphasized the health benefits of outdoor recreation, the opportunities afforded for scientific research, the tourism appeal of the lake and the effectiveness of game protection regulations within the park. The Canadian National Railway, the Grand Trunk Pacific, the Alpine Club of Canada and the Campfire Club of America joined the fight to convince the government to re-extend the park boundaries to include Maligne Lake. On June 14, 1914, Jasper Park was restored to 4,400 square miles (11,396 square kilometres), including Maligne Lake. How close we came to losing that "string of pearls" from the protection of National Parks.

Time to Tarry-a-while

No, the cemetery is anything but bothering.
It is a place of rest, kindly neighbors and
a harbinger of birds during the summer.
—Mary Schäffer, 1933[73]

Mary found her times of greatest peace and pleasure in the West. As the contrast between the

[Mrs. Caroline Sharpless and Paul Sharpless with boat on shore of Maligne Lake, 1911]

MARY SCHÄFFER FONDS (V527/PS 1 – 139)

freedom she experienced on the trail and the pressures of society became increasingly more irritating, Mary began dreaming of "a home in the west, where [she] could go out, saddle [her] pony and ride among the hills."[74] For a few years she extended her mountain visits into the winter months. Finally, in 1911, she decided to relocate. In the fall of that year, with the help of Billy Warren, Mary obtained a lot in Banff and had her home, called Tarry-a-while, built.

In 1912 Mary moved into her new home, her first permanent residence since Charles Schäffer's death. Three years later, on June 24, 1915, she married Billy Warren, her guide and beloved "Chief." Mary's first husband, Charles, had been more than 20 years her senior. Billy was nearly 20

Tarry-a-while, Banff, Alberta, Whyte Museum of the Canadian Rockies, n.d.

years her junior. Despite the age difference and rumours about Billy's exploits, the two shared a life of mutual support and ongoing friendship.

Mary and William Warren were both very active members of their community. During the First World War, Mary contributed to Banff's war effort by knitting socks, corresponding with

Mary Schäffer in her home [Tarry-a-while], c1920

soldiers and even sending a lantern-slide show to wounded soldiers in Britain. In early 1919 she joined the local chapter of the Imperial Order Daughters of the Empire, where she strongly supported the drive to erect a monument to Banff's fallen soldiers. Mary also donated her time to various fundraising projects for St. George's-in-the-Pines Anglican Church.

With Mary's assistance, Billy adapted his guiding business to the needs of motor tourists. In 1919 he cofounded the Cascade Garage and Banff Motor Company. Two years later, he and partner James McLeod acquired the King Edward livery business and converted it into the Rocky Mountain Tours & Transport Company. Billy was an entrepreneur who sought to make it on his own, and although Mary's personal savings helped him to get started, he had a keen business sense and became independently successful.

By the 1930s, Mary declared herself "quite sick of old folks," even though by this time she was in her seventies.[75] Having no children of her own, Mary enjoyed the company of Banff's youth. Banff's young adults considered her a second mother. They spoke fondly of her generous hospitality, took her out dancing, and congregated at Tarry-a-while for weekly bridge nights. She never tired of visits from her brothers and their families, old friends like the Vaux family and newer ones like R.B. Bennett and climber Lillian Gest. She loved to advise newcomers on the best routes through the mountains and was keen to learn and share all she could about alpine history.

Throughout her time in Banff, Mary continued to pursue her interest in photography, capturing the surrounding mountains, lakes and daily life. Mary included several photographs of Cascade Mountain in Part I of her lantern slide presentation: "It stretches a long distance to the north and in it is embedded large masses of coal, some of which have been mined."[76] Mary also refers to Bankhead: "There is a drive of nine miles to it [Lake Minnewanka], when one passes the animal pastures and goes through the departing village of Bankhead, once a thriving mining village." Bankhead existed from 1904 to 1922 to mine coal on the eastern slopes of Cascade Mountain.

Mary includes a number of images of the Banff Buffalo or Animal Paddock. The Banff Buffalo Paddock originated in 1898 to protect a few surviving examples of the near-extinct plains bison that had been donated to the national park. "Buffalo" is the colloquial name for bison. By 1909 the bison herd had grown to 107. The Buffalo Paddock, as it became known, eventually kept live specimens of most of the wild mammals found at that time in the Rocky Mountain parks. The paddock was a popular tourist attraction. The bison herd remained in the paddock until 1997, when the last ten animals and the fences containing them were removed to improve the wildlife corridor along the north side of the Bow Valley.[77]

In Part I of her slide presentation, Mary highlights a strange little anomaly regarding the Buffalo Paddock. She includes images of baby moose that were destined for New Zealand. She remarks:

Time after time moose had been asked for by New Zealand. The animals always succumbed before reaching their destination. At last someone decided to try baby moose. Though very young they were raised on bottles, brought to Banff where they were as tame as the family cat, and so far as was ever learned they reached the far-away country for which they had been raised.[78]

This was clearly a time before the introduction of non-native species was understood to be as detrimental as it is today.

Mary documented some aspects of daily life in Banff that she found photogenic or interesting as a transplant to the area. For example, ice-harvesting is one of the activities she photographed and included in Part I of her lantern slide presentation. Prior to the invention of the refrigerator, ice houses were buildings that were used to store ice throughout the year. They were extremely well insulated, which ensured that ice harvested in the winter months would remain frozen. During the winter months, ice was chopped from a river or lake surface and often dragged by sledge to the ice house. Mary shows the ice harvest in Banff. H.T. Cummings, author of an article entitled "Ice: Its Collection, Storage and Distribution," wrote that "when the season has been favourable, and the ice has attained the requisite thickness, – the thicker the better, – the ice men proceed to work. As horsepower is much employed, and as ice less than five inches in thickness will not bear the weight of a horse, in an open winter it is sometimes late before the ice cutters can commence operations."[79] As ice became more available, the demand for it increased as well. By 1879 there were 35 commercial ice plants in America, more than 200 a decade later and 2,000 by 1909. In 1907, 14 to 15 million tons of ice was consumed, which was nearly triple the amount in 1880.[80] In summer months ice was delivered from local ice houses to residences in ice wagons or ice trucks, where it would be stored in an icebox, which was used much like a modern refrigerator. Iceboxes were typically made of wood, lined with tin or zinc and insulated with sawdust or seaweed.

In Part I of her slideshow, Mary also includes a winter photograph of the Upper Hot Springs in Banff. In an unpublished article, "The Byways of Banff," she sings the praises of Banff's winter:

The atmosphere is dry and invigorating, the high winds of the prairies pass us by, it is very easy to keep warm in Banff. Skating begins in November and lasts about four months. Ice boating can be had on Lake Minnewanka. Sleighing usually begins in December and lasts till the end of March. The toboggan slide is always to hand and bathing in the hot sulphur pools under the open sky, a delightful and novel experience, while ski-ing and snow-shoeing may be added to the long list of pleasant things to do. Taking all things into consideration, for anyone who loves the out-of-door life, Banff has no season when it is ever dull.[81]

Photographs of many winter activities appear in her lantern-slide shows.

Mary enjoyed her life in Banff, but as she grew older, she mourned the loss of the wilderness areas she loved. As roads were built, the areas where only First Nations people and those with a great sense of adventure and courage had ventured only a few years earlier were becoming easier to access by the ever-increasing influx of tourists. Mary's slides capture a time when life seemed simpler.

Tobogganing at Banff, n.d.

(V527/PS I – 261)

THE HISTORY AND TECHNOLOGY OF LANTERN SLIDES

The coloring of lantern-slides is not a difficult task, but it is necessary that they be handled with great care, as the film is very delicate and easily spoiled.
—*J.B. Schriever*[82]

Lantern slides, often called "magic lantern" slides, originated in the late 1600s in Europe. However, the mainstream introduction of lantern slides in 1849, ten years after the invention of photography, allowed photographs to be viewed in an entirely new format. As a transparent slide projected onto a surface, the photograph could be seen not only by individuals and small groups but also by a larger audience.

Hyalotype was the name given to lantern slides using photographs. Two daguerreotypists in Philadelphia, William and Frederick Langenheim, invented this technology in 1849. At this time lantern slides were black and white, but they were frequently tinted with transparent colours to enhance their effect on the screen. There were various types of magic lantern slide projectors available: single-lens; double-lens, or "stereopticon," projectors; magic lantern projectors; even a triple-lens machine that could produce even fancier effects.

A magic lantern consists of seven functional sections: the lamp, reflector, condensing lens, lens tube, body, base and smokestack. The lamp provides the sole source of illumination, fuelled by burning oil or gas, a piece of calcium or, later, electricity. The reflector bounces the light from the lamp toward the condensing lens, which then focuses the beam onto the slide being projected. The lens tube serves to magnify the illuminated slide, so that projected images from 1.8 metres (6 feet) to 3.6 metres (12 feet) wide can be obtained. The body of the machine is often made completely of metal, and it houses all of the components except the lens tube. The base lifts the magic lantern above the surface of a table. This is important because, once running, the body of the machine becomes intensely hot from the illuminating lamp (the base helps to prevent table burns).

Mary Schäffer's lantern slide projector, circa early 1900s[83]

The magic lantern reached its peak in popularity in the 1880s and 1890s. They were almost as common in middle-class homes as television sets or computers are today. The most impressive professional shows in Europe involved as many as eight projection operators at one time and attracted up to 2,000 people per show. At the turn of the 20th century, the introduction of the cinema and of photo reproduction in newspapers brought about a decline in the use of magic lanterns. In Britain the industry died by the 1920s. However, in distant corners of the British Commonwealth, including Western Canada, magic-lantern use persisted until the 1930s.[84]

Besides the photographic medium itself, the process for creating lantern slides remained primarily the same throughout its 100-year history. There were two ways of printing the images: the contact method, and the camera method. The first dictated placing the negative directly on the light-sensitive glass. This required that the negative be the correct size to produce the 8.9 cm (3.5 inch) × 10.2 cm (4 inch) slide. For larger negatives, the camera method was necessary. Using a camera with a long bed and bellows, the negative and glass were both placed in the camera and printed by exposing the glass to daylight or artificial light. After exposure in both cases, the latent image was developed with chemicals. After the plate was dried, the image could be hand-coloured using special tints. The slide was finished with a mat and a glass cover and taped to seal the enclosure.[85]

Mary's Lantern Slides

Mary used lantern slides so that she might share her love of the Canadian Rockies with others. Although she began as a talented watercolour artist, her neuralgia made it increasingly difficult for her to paint, so she developed her talent in photography and hand-tinting lantern slides.

Philadelphia was known as "the lantern slide capital of America."[86] Having lived there for much of her life, it is only natural that Mary would make use of this technology.

With many of Mary's lantern slides, the paper masks – the mat that frames each image – bear the name Charles R. Pancoast. This could mean one of two things. Mary may have had some of her photographs processed in Philadelphia by Charles R. Pancoast or it is possible she simply ordered blank glass sheets and paper mats with the Pancoast imprint. As mentioned earlier, Mary hand-tinted many of her slides, adding transparent colour pigments to her original black and white positive transparencies to create colour slides.

Although most of the slides included in this book were photographs taken by Mary or her travelling companions, some were purchased or acquired by trade with other photographers and then hand-coloured by Mary. It appears she acquired some black and white transparencies from

The mask, or mat, used to surround a lantern slide image

Mary Schäffer's Pony Premo folding camera, circa early 1900s

Banff photographer Byron Harmon. She then hand-coloured these slides herself. She also purchased slides from H.C. White Co. and T.H. McAllister, Manufacturing Optician, both of 49 Nassau Street, New York. It is likely that she hand-coloured these images also, but it is also possible they were coloured when she purchased them.

Manuals of the time, such as Schriever's *Complete Self-Instructing Library of Practical Photography*, gave explicit instructions on how to colour lantern slides:

Before applying any colors the whole surface of the plate should be moistened with clean water. Holding the slide with the head toward you, with a large brush well filled with water, moisten the whole surface of the plate. Work up the background first. Take the medium sized brush, moderately charged with weak color, and wash the background evenly in long strokes. Continue applying the weak color until the correct density and shade

are obtained. Wash over large spaces as quickly as possible, so they will not be streaked or spotted. If difficulty should be experienced along this line, reduce by applying, with the brush, water or 95% alcohol....

For all lantern-slide work, the strongest and most brilliant colors are not only desirable, but necessary, and it is important that the very best make of colors be secured, for the strong light of the lantern

Mary Schäffer's paintbox with oil paint tubes, circa early 1900s

will fade them after they have been in use for some time, if the colors are not sufficiently pure to withstand the action of the light….

A white card, laid back of the slide while coloring, will show small details perfectly.[87]

Although the manuals touted the ease of hand-colouring lantern slides, the craft required care and attention to detail. To do it well also required artistry. Mary's artistic eye made the slides artworks in themselves. Her style is clear in her use of soft colours and delicate washes.

The three images entitled "Formosa Savage on the trail" illustrate the process of hand-colouring lantern slides. The first image is the black and white transparency. The other two are duplicates of the same image, but Mary has coloured each of them differently.

Formosa Savage on the trail, 1908

MARY SCHÄFFER FONDS LEFT (V527/PS I – 991), CENTRE (V527/PS I – 1045), RIGHT (V527/PS I – 911)

It is remarkable that so many of Mary's fragile glass lantern slides have survived. During her lifetime they were used for many different purposes, from presentations to attract tourists to the Canadian Rockies to slideshows for soldiers overseas during the First World War. It was during the war that Mary lost both her nephew Eric Sharpless and her dear friend Sid Unwin, which brought the conflict home for her. Understanding the importance of home to soldiers convalescing in British hospitals, Mary developed a lantern-slide show for them entitled "In the Heart of the Canadian Rockies with Horse and Camera." Mary recognized her slides had great impact. She notes that one young soldier wrote, "I had a splendid night last night. Was wheeled into the assembly hall of the hospital and there were the photos of Banff; it was dark enough that the other fellows did not see the tears. It made me pretty homesick, but I am getting along alright and will soon be back."[88]

The lantern slides Mary selected for her presentations and the stories that accompany them tell us a great deal about her: her love of the wilderness, her interest in botany, her sympathy for animals and her sadness at witnessing how life was changing for First Nations people. Mary's sense of humour also comes through loud and clear in her lantern slide presentations. She was not afraid to exaggerate some of her stories, or to have a laugh at her own expense. She loved exploring the backcountry and it was this passion and her natural curiosity that led her from one place to the next. She strongly encouraged others, particularly women, to follow in her footsteps.

The next two chapters in this book reproduce each of Mary's Canadian Rockies slideshows. All of the text accompanying the slides, with the exception of that in square brackets, is taken from Mary's "In the Heart of the Canadian Rockies with Horse and Camera, Part I," and "In the Heart of the Canadian Rockies with Horse and Camera,

Part II: At the Head Waters of the Saskatchewan and Athabaska: A Sequel to 'In the Heart of the Canadian Rockies.'" All of the photographs and artifacts are from the Whyte Museum of the Canadian Rockies' collections. Most of the original slides used in Mary's talks have become part of the Whyte's collection, and these slides have been included. Where slides were missing, broken or not identified, I have taken the liberty of replacing them with other slides from Mary's collection that fit the text. If an appropriate slide could not be found in her collection, I have, as often as possible, used slides attributed to her from other Whyte Museum resources such as the Moore and the Lonsdale collections. The Moores and Lonsdales were friends of Mary's and they would often exchange slides when producing presentations. All of their collections now reside in the Whyte Museum's Archives. Any changes or additions are identified with an asterisk. In Part I, Mary uses titles for many of her slides, but not all. In Part II, she does not use any. Although this may be somewhat confusing, I have left the titles where they appeared in the original scripts.

IN THE HEART OF THE CANADIAN ROCKIES WITH HORSE AND CAMERA, PART I

by Mary S. Warren, Banff, Alberta

I. MAP OF CANADA AND UNITED STATES

To get even a limited idea of that of which one speaks in geographical language, that tedious thing – a map – must be inserted. The one shown gives a suggestion of Canada and the United States and the position of that great transcontinental road, the Canadian Pacific, which was the pioneer of all roads on this side of the line. It was a much mooted question as to whether such a feat as a continuous road through Canada could ever be accomplished and those who felt they understood conditions had much to contend with from the public both in Canada and England. The shores of the Great Lakes must have been a heart breaking task, with their trestles and tunnels and bridges, and the constantly falling rocks, but still there was nothing impossible about the work. As for the long wide plains, they were comparatively easy to overcome; it was the long stretch of mountainous country which Captain John Palliser of England found a terrible proposition. He remained in the country from '59 to '65, and in his report to the home government was forced to admit that unless the road could be partly run through the States the test could not be accomplished. All of this may be read in that rare book known as "Palliser's report", but the writer once had the good fortune of learning at first hand how it happened that a part of the expedition penetrated as far as Golden and later went north of the present [Lake] Louise station to the Bow Lake.

Like many another thing accomplished, it came by accident. Sir James Hector, then Dr. Hector of the Palliser party[,] was visiting Canada in 1903, was stopping at Glacier and was announcing to an interested listener that "he meant to see his grave before returning to New Zealand – his home for the latter part of his life." This being a rather astonishing statement, he was asked just what he meant. "Well," said the old pioneer, "You see I was over here with Palliser as physician. We simply could go no farther west than the Indians permitted. They felt we were after their hunting country and that ended it. It looked as though all our efforts were to be in vain, and there were the Rockies stretched right before us. Dysentery broke out in the camp of the Indians which was close to us. I took over a few simple remedies, changed their camp, got everyone well, and after that I could have anything I wanted. We entered the Valley of the Bow, climbed a mountain which is now called Cascade, went over Vermilion Pass, reached what is now so well known as Windermere country, and came back down the Columbia where the present village of Golden now stands. Seeing a large stream coming from the east, we made our way up it. It was terrible traveling as we had to take to the steep hillsides. Coming up a very wild stream I decided to cross it to the other side. My horse never did have a good disposition, so I was insisting that he get into that water and over. He was just as certain he was not going. I went for him from the rear when he bowled me over so badly the rest of the party

thought I was dead. We did things in a hurry in those days so they dug my grave, but fortunately I came to just as they were going to bury me. I know I could find the hole. We named the river the Kicking Horse and I am going to find the place."

He never did. His brilliant young son Douglas, who had accompanied his father to the land of his parent's youthful work, died suddenly at Revelstoke and lies there today, the place marked by a fine granite stone. The broken father bowed his head to grief and fate and returned to New Zealand, to pass away a few years later. Such briefly is the history of the first attempt to lay a road of steel across the continent, at least of Canada. Others had gone before Sir James, but not for this special purpose. As the prairies are an old story to everyone who has passed across the country we will plunge at once into the most scenic part of the "Great Playground of the North."

Map of Canada and United States

MARY SCHÄFFER FONDS (V527/PS 2 – 1)

RAILWAY MAP
OF THE
UNITED STATES

Scale of Miles

Railroads ——— Through Routes ———

2. BANFF

Banff became a village in the days of construction of the great highway and was originally located where now the elk and buffalo roam. Later, owing to the location of the hotel and the presence of fine sulphur springs, the village today sprang up in the heart of the hills.[89]

74

W. [West] fr [from] "Tunnel" Banff [after 1915]

MARY SCHÄFFER FONDS (V527/PS 2 – 2)

[Bow River near Banff]

(v439/ps – 211)*

3. MOUNT RUNDLE

Here Mount Rundle is shown with the Bow River in the foreground. This mountain received its name [from] the Rev. Dr. Rundle who as far back as 1840 had left his placid home in England to work among the Indians. The writer has the only memo he ever left. His was the salvation of a savage race whom he found gentle and kindly. In his diary he seldom speaks of the beauty of the foothills where he apparently was located most of the time, but occasionally he mentions the great mountains shining in the sun or bathed in clouds and one morning he decided he would take a walk over to the mountains and obtain a stone to take home to England as a souvenir. He adds, "I walked all day and apparently was no nearer, and through fatigue was forced to go back to my camp without the stone." So clear is the atmosphere in the Canadian mountains one can easily understand how such a great mistake was made by a stranger.

Mt. [Mount Rundle]

MOORE FAMILY FONDS
(V439/PS – 205)*

4. GOAT MOUNTAIN

Swinging the camera a little to the south of the last picture, Goat Mountain comes into view. This mountain lies in the upper valley of the Spray River and is about 8 miles south of Banff. The waters of the Spray River have their rise in the lakes of the same name and consequently the Spray River is almost invariably clear. Considerably further south than this mountain is the "White Man's Pass," that pass over which Father De Smet crossed long before the days of the Palliser expedition. Like [Rev.] Dr. Rundle he probably thought far more of the souls he had come to claim than of scenery. Sixteen miles up the Spray River there is an opening in the hills which leads down to the mining town of Canmore and which now is frequently given the name of the above pass, but it is a misnomer and misleading.

To Goat Mountain from Bow Valley

MARY SCHÄFFER FONDS (V527/PS 2 – 4)

5. BOW VALLEY

The camera turned due west shows the range of hills from which flows the Bow River; in the foreground is that river. No one seems to know the origin of the name unless it was given by someone noticing the winding, tortuous path through the long valleys. A slight glimpse of the public boathouse may be seen where, in summer, fussy little naphtha[90] launches play back and forth beneath the frowning mountains and in the winter the snow is kept swept away from those who spend their time skating or in games of hockey.

1026. MASSIVE RANGE FROM BRIDGE.

Massive Range from bridge

BYRON HARMON FONDS (V263/NA – 4440)*

6. SAXIFRAGA NUTKANA

One of the earliest flowers to bloom about Banff is the little Saxifraga Nutkana. It stands about ten inches high, grows in white masses and has the delicious odor of "sweet grass" for which Indians are noted for making baskets. As the season advances it blooms at higher and higher levels till at last it has been found at the summit of Sulphur Mountain.

Saxifraga levcanthemifolia

MARY SCHÄFFER FONDS (527/PSI – 537)

[Mary labelled this image *Saxifraga levcanthemifolia*, but its appearance is very similar to the *Saxifraga nutkana*, which is now called *Saxifraga micranthes*.]

Alpine Anemone

MOORE FAMILY FONDS
(V439/PS – 242)*

7. ALPINE ANEMONE

The Alpine Anemone, or Pulsatilla, is found only in the higher reaches of the mountains. It is a creamy white. Its purple sister is found in large quantities in the lower valleys and is often called the "wind flower" – an attractive name for the bright blossom which is never still in the constant winds which come down the valleys. As the petals die away, the seed-pods are almost equally attractive and with small imagination one might call them "hairy little men of the hills."

Alpine Anemone [with seed pods]

LONSDALE FONDS (V368/PS – 243)*

8. CASCADE MOUNTAIN

Cascade Mountain, named for a stream of water which flows permanently on its eastern face, was probably one of the first mountains in this vicinity ever to be climbed by a white man. Sir James Hector is supposed to have made at least a partial ascent to locate valleys and passes whereby he could penetrate the hills to the west. It stretches a long distance to the north and in it are embedded large masses of coal, some of which will be mined.

Cascade Mountain [Charles Leroy with cow on Banff Avenue, 1886]

MARY SCHÄFFER FONDS (V527/PS 1 – 233)*

9. [AND 10. JOINED TOGETHER] STONEY INDIANS

The Stoney Indians of the foothills still return year by year to their old hunting grounds, but under vastly different conditions. Today their costumes are still brilliant with imported beads, the buckskin of former years is almost gone. There are no buffalo hide teepees, few soft skin garments, just gay prints[,] cheap ribbons, and until recently a very poor type of blanket. The glamour of the Aborigine is departing. He feels it. Where he once stepped a proud, free man, the wild creatures of the hills his for the hunting, he comes now as a ward of the government. The old men of the tribes pass on to the younger generation the stories of the glory of the past. It is tragedy at our door.

Stoney Indians

MARY SCHÄFFER FONDS (V527/PS 2 – 9 AND 10)

II. INDIAN FAMILY

To date the Indian has not adopted the motor car and there is something pathetically funny in seeing their faces when they pick up a taxi on that now well-established "Indian Day" at Banff and go rushing back to their camp about a mile from the village. The love of their horses will probably go with them as long as any of their tribe is left. The "Squaw Race" is one of the great events, the girls decked in yards of vari-colored[91] ribbons and gorgeous prints fly around the track with as great excitement as any of their men friends. This little family is dressed for the parade which always preceded the sports at their regular camp.

Indian Family

MARY SCHÄFFER FONDS (V527/PS 2 – II)

12. NATIVE CAMP

As they live in their native state
– when tourists are numerous in
August and where many people from
outlying districts come to behold this
fast-departing glimpse of the old
days on the plains among the Indians.

Native Camp

MARY SCHÄFFER FONDS (V527/PS 2 – 12)

13. UPPER HOT SPRINGS

One of the great attractions of Banff, both for pleasure and health, is the number of swimming pools of strong sulphur water. The largest are the Upper Hot Springs where one may bathe in dead of winter, the Middle Springs which are much less pretentious and the Cave and Basin where a large swimming pool has been built by the government at great cost, with dressing rooms, etc. The original pool bursts from the mountain side and is walled in artificially, thus making swimming in that part of the basin practicable the entire year. During the winter carnival which has now become an annual affair, races take place in the larger pool between the children of the village and visitors. The picture shown was taken at the Upper Hot Springs during a cold snap. The steam rising from the naturally heated water makes a marvelous festoon of ice and so great is the heat of the water that one may bathe with impunity at 10 or 20 below zero [Fahrenheit].

Upper Hot Springs

MARY SCHÄFFER FONDS (V527/PS I – 260)*

14.

The wild animals at the Banff National Park are a great attraction to visitors. So long have they been protected from the hunter that they scarcely know the least fear. The buffalo is an exception and it takes the greatest watchfulness on the part of the caretaker of the herd to keep the stranger from climbing from his car to get a closer snap-shot of the lazy-looking brutes. A fence is a good safe place from which to take a picture, for the buffalo has ever been known to resent a car coming into his pasture. He is not the least bit afraid, it is the tourist who has usually not enough imagination to know that protection has taught the Monarch of the Plains he has nothing to fear from man.

The Buffalo

MARY SCHÄFFER FONDS (DAMAGED) (V527/PS 2 – 14)

15. BUFFALO

The herd at Banff is very limited owing to the small range, but at Wainwright is now gathered the last of the great herd of the continent. (In 1939 this herd was disbanded.) It was known as the Pablo herd, a private one owned in the United States. It took infinite trouble and care to bring the buffalo across the line but time and patience did it all.

Buffalo

MARY SCHÄFFER FONDS
(V527/PS 2 – 15)

16. ELK

Quite close to the buffalo is the elk pasture. These beautiful creatures may be seen in large numbers after sunset in the summer enjoying browsing in the open, for with the sunset depart the flies which annoy them exceedingly. The male is an especially handsome creature, stalking with masculine vanity amidst his harem. Quite recently a large number of the elk have been placed in the open range and one may catch a glimpse of them occasionally as a car glides swiftly by, but they are perhaps the most shy wild animals of the mountains living under protection.

**Elk in Nat. [National]
Park, Banff, Alberta**

17. MOOSE

The moose also is kept for visitors to
see, but his unfortunate temperament
makes him as difficult to reach as the
buffalo, except that he clings to the
brush and no car can reach his habitat. The accompanying photo was
taken with a good-sized tree behind
the photographer, but as she is no
climber, I am not just sure why she
worried about having a tree at all.

Moose

MARY SCHÄFFER FONDS
(V527/PS 2 – 17)

18. MOUNTAIN SHEEP

The mountain sheep have probably responded to the protection which the government has afforded to all the wild animals in the national parks better than any other species. A few years ago it took days to hunt them in their natural haunts; today the thousands of motor cars plying on the [Lake] Louise road are sure to pass group after group browsing beside the road, bending to the salt-licks or coming from the drinking places. The Louise road is the haunt of the wild sheep and their tameness has caused immense pleasure to those who have never before had the privilege of seeing them so close.

Two Mountain Sheep

MARY SCHÄFFER FONDS (V527/PS I – 456)*

19. MOUNTAIN SHEEP

In this picture one sheep stands listening to the coming of a vehicle and two more are directly on the skyline slowly browsing their way over to the other side of the low hill. In the spring the ewes wander about with their young lambs and the yearlings follow closely along. The rams, ungallant creatures, leaving the ladies to look after the families, wander back into the fastnesses of the hills. When fall arrives they once more return to the bosom of the home. Not for peace, however, for no sooner do they appear than trouble starts and it is the survival of the fittest. Fighting seems to be the order of the day. Traveling along quietly on the highway one frequently hears the smashing and crashing of horns as two enormous heads come together to settle some family dispute. Hunters have frequently reported finding skulls of sheep locked together. Fighting, they had become entangled and died of starvation.

Rocky Mountain Sheep

MARY SCHÄFFER FONDS (V527/PS 1 – 457)*

20. ANTELOPE

This picture of the antelope was taken a number of years ago and probably could never be obtained today. They are gentle little creatures, not at all shy in captivity but captivity cannot hold them. They seem to be migratory in habit and several years ago when the Canadian Pacific Railway fenced off miles of country where the antelope were plentiful the writer has seen them by hundreds lying dead by the fences they could not pass. They were headed south but the southland could not be reached. All the care lavished on them in their park home could not save the gentle little creatures. They are all dead.

[Antelope, Buffalo Paddock, Banff]

MARY SCHÄFFER FONDS (V527/PS 1 – 446)*

21. BABY MOOSE

This photo also will probably never be repeated. Time after time moose had been asked for by New Zealand. The animals always succumbed before reaching their destination. At last someone decided to try baby moose. Though very young they were raised on bottles, brought to Banff where they were as tame as the family cat, and so far as was ever learned they reached the far-away country for which they had been raised. These little fellows are about three years old. They are of very slow growth and seem to remain infants till at least fifteen years of age.

Baby Moose in Banff Nat. [National] Park

MARY SCHÄFFER FONDS (V527/PS I – 490)*

22. BOW RIVER AT SUNSET

Bow River at Sunset

A glimpse of the Bow River at the setting of the sun. So deep is the vista, so long the range, the camera can almost depend daily on this spot for a subject. Anyone unaccustomed to the rigors of our northern climate would scarce believe there were times when a breeze reaching fifty below zero could sweep down these green valleys but we of the northland know it is all too common.

23. BOW RIVER IN WINTER — ICE HARVEST

This photo is of the winter harvest of ice in the valley previously shown. The Bow River becomes a river of ice about 30 or 38 inches thick and not till then does the cutting take place. People accustomed to lower altitudes and seaboards look with horror on a climate where the mercury takes such liberties. The cold may become a little tiresome, but those who have tried both high and low altitudes generally assert they suffer far less with cold in dry climates than in moist.

Bow River in Winter – Ice Harvest

MARY SCHÄFFER FONDS (V527/PS 2 – 23)

Mountaineering is one of the sports of this section as well as throughout the mountains generally. For those who are fond of it, it holds out innumerable inducements. The first requisite is a steady head and second a full supply of nerves which will not play false to their owner at a critical moment.

Mountaineering

25.

After a long rough climb in brush, the sight of ice is welcome. Then goggles are adjusted[,] for the glare of surrounding whiteness is apt to cause snow-blindness, something which is decidedly to be avoided as an experience, as the writer can confirm. Stout boots are worn. No frills are attached to climbing togs, too dangerous is it that something catch on rock or other obstruction.

Mountaineering

MARY SCHÄFFER FONDS, PHOTOGRAPHER BYRON HARMON (V527/PS 2 – 25)*

26. ASCENT OF MT. WILCOX

Then the rope is attached to every member of the party, the professional guides taking their places according to the strength of the party. It is never safe for untried climbers to attack high mountains or snowfields without a thoroughly tried and understanding guide – thus may trouble be avoided. The photo shows the last part of Wilcox Pass. It is not at all difficult as such performances go, but the writer never had further desire to try any sort of mountain again. Near the summit no rope was being used as the leader seemed to think it was very easy. Following closely at his heels, she suddenly lost him and was sure he had taken a short cut to the bottom without making a noise. That drop was all of one thousand feet. She glanced around the corner of a rock and there he was waving her imperatively to come ahead. I assure you there was a ledge between the two which was not more than two feet wide, five yards long and a sheer drop to the valley far below. What do we not do for fear of being laughed at; that fear carried her over the horrid space with head held high, teeth bitten into lips and a vow in her heart to look at things later from a lower level. That vow was never broken. There are still mountains and mountains which have never yet been scaled and which afford a "first ascent" so vast is the great chain of our own inimitable Rockies. Once an Englishman who had trotted the globe over was asked the usual question, "how do you like our Rockies?" I wish I could include the tone and the accent, but that being impossible I can give only the idea. "Oh, I do not care for them at all. One climbs and climbs and there are still more mountains to climb. If I were in

Switzerland I could finish them all up in a short
time, but a man's whole life would not permit his
finishing the Canadian Rockies."

100

Mountaineering

LONSDALE FONDS
(v368/ps 2 – 444)*

27. [AND 28. JOINED TOGETHER]
SNOWFIELDS NEAR THE SUMMIT

This photo shows the last snowfields before the summit is reached. Ice axes have come into action. It looks very easy but ears are ever alert for the sound of cracking ice which betokens a coming avalanche – the breathing becomes laboured with the high altitude. Some love the sport – but – some do not. But there are compensations. The magnificent views, the purity of the snows, the wonderful silence, the glissades when the hardest work is over, when there are a few moments to turn to the great blue-green grottos of ice, and relaxing a few moments [to] let every tired muscle rest, rest in the wonderful coloring of which this is but a

Snowfields near the Summit

MARY SCHÄFFER FONDS,
PHOTOGRAPHER BYRON HARMON
(V527/PS 2 – 27)

meek sample. Yes, it does pay, even if you are scared beyond expression – a fright you may confide to no-one. I like to hear the real alpinists talk, I know so well they leave out a lot and nothing will convince me that they do not.

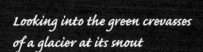

Looking into the green crevasses of a glacier at its snout

MARY SCHÄFFER FONDS,
PHOTOGRAPHER BYRON HARMON
(V527/PS 2 – 28)

29. NEARING THE GOAL

This photo shows our party slowly but surely reaching the goal, the summit of a 12,000 ft. Mountain. What matter it where? The struggle, the scramble, the weariness begun at dawn, are almost ended. It takes one who goes on such a jaunt to appreciate the coming of the end especially if he has gone under protest as the writer has done a number of times.

Nearing the Goal

MARY SCHÄFFER FONDS, PHOTOGRAPHER BYRON HARMON (V527/PS 2 – 29)

30.

There are a few last panting struggles, and these may be written in huge letters, especially if the climber has a quivery spot around the second button of his vest or she has a palpitation around the third button of her neat khaki shirt. I won't believe that men and women vary very much at a high altitude. It is only the guide who counts after all. It is he who stiffens doubting legs and strengthens a weakening will.

Nearing the Goal

MARY SCHÄFFER FONDS
(V527/PS 2 – 30)

31. THE SUMMIT

At last the summit is
there – crunched under foot, de-
spised for the moment and admired
the next. But all the same I am will-
ing to admit that to gaze at that
comb of snow from a winter fire-
place is exceedingly satisfactory.

The Summit

MARY SCHÄFFER FONDS,
PHOTOGRAPHER BYRON HARMON
(V527/PS 2 – 31)

Here the descent has begun. There is a feeling of thankfulness that the peak at last has been surmounted and done with for the day. There is an inclination to sing and to feel that troubles are all over, when an ugly thought intrudes. There is the descent when the day warmed to the summer sun. There is an ice bridge to cross, will it hold? There are crevasses to cross which may have weakened in the heat. Going down, someone dandles out of sight, is fished up with bruises aplenty and the rest of the novices scared stiff. A glissade is made, when one's garments are filled with snow, and speaking feelingly there is one human being who is quite willing for the other fellow to find all the glory he can in first or last ascents. The one great ascent is wonderful, but does it pay?

And so it goes on, bridges and crevasses follow one another in monotonous succession. The struggle of climbing ceases with the ascent, but the struggle against the day's heat on the weak ice leaves no mental misery in doubt for the unprofessional climber, that climber who is scared from start to finish. Yet there are thousands of people who SAY it is the most wonderful sport. They may have it all; personally I think they have a few mental reservations of which they do not speak.

Above: The Descent

MARY SCHÄFFER FONDS
(DAMAGED) (V527/PS 2 – 33)

Opposite: The Descent

MARY SCHÄFFER FONDS
(DAMAGED) (V527/PS 2 – 32)

34. LAKE MINNEWANKA, OR DEVIL'S LAKE

Among the interesting outlying environs of Banff is Lake Minnewanka, known locally as Devil's Lake. Perhaps this name was derived from the sudden squalls or storms which sweep down on the lake without much warning. There is a drive of nine miles to it, when one passes the animal pastures and goes through the departing village of Bankhead, once a thriving mining village. Surrounded by high mountains, Mt. Aylmer is yet the highest and is accessible to climbers. In the summer a stout little boat plies the waters of the lake, and in the winter ice-boating is very good. Formerly its shores were the route into the hills for hunting but since a motor road links Calgary and Banff they now use the easier way. Many years ago we were driving to the lake when we suddenly beheld quite a party of Indians coming our way. The writer was utterly "green." Frightened of the savages (?) and when the driver said "jump" she was out of that rig before the word was right out.

The Indians took in the situation, politely dropped down into the gully, grunted "How," laughed and the incident was closed. But never again had the Indians any terror for the easterner, the smiles made us friends, a friendship which continues to this day.

Lake Minnewanka, or Devil's Lake, nine miles from Banff, Alberta

MARY SCHÄFFER FONDS (DAMAGED) (V527/PS 2 – 34)

35. MOUNT BALL

Mount Ball is comparatively near to Banff, and lies to the southwest of the village. Its summit can be distinctly seen from the general motor highway. It ranks as one of the higher mountains, and its summit is permanently covered with snow. It is a scenic mountain from every point and is worthy of those who are fond of climbing.

Mount Ball

MARY SCHÄFFER FONDS,
PHOTOGRAPHER BYRON HARMON (V527/PS 2 – 35)

36. LAKE LOUISE

The government has at last linked up the roads which make a transcontinental highway, but the road to Louise was finished first and has been used by motorists for some time. The distance is about 38 miles, not including the side trip to Moraine Lake district, but the whole may be made from Banff very easily in one day. From the time the lake was discovered (back in the eighties), it has been known as one of the most beautiful scenic districts. Lake Louise is only about one mile long, is about two and a half miles from the station of the same name and is worth the visit. At one time a small chalet stood at the border of the lake; it was burned down, then came a place of larger dimensions at the foot of the lake, built by the CPR. Every convenience under the sun may be found in the heart of the wilderness. Ponies carry people to the higher lakes, Mirror and Agnes, small tea houses have sprung up, at least 100 miles of trail ramify every interesting point so one may be happy at Louise for weeks if climbing, walking, strange flowers, etc., will call them there. There is a wonderful walking trip over the ice of Mt. Victoria to Lake O'Hara (named for one of the earlier surveyors) and it is well worth the trip.

Lake Louise and Victoria Glacier

MARY SCHÄFFER FONDS (V527/PS 2 – 36)

37. VIEW TAKEN TO THE RIGHT OF THE LAST

This picture was taken more to the right of the last one and Mt. Victoria has disappeared from view. Mt. Lefroy comes more prominently into view and the forefront of Mt. Fairview. During the summer both mountains send down avalanches in the hottest part of the day which are very impressive and also beautiful as they crash in tons and tons of ice into the valleys below. For the botanist there is no larger field to work in perfect comfort than Chateau Lake Louise. Saxifrages are there in enormous quantities, the false forget-me-nots, arnicas, etc., and in June the Lyall's larch may be found blooming in the deep snows about 8,000 ft. high, and a little later the snow lilies and pulsatilla. It is a botanist's paradise.

Lake Louise

MARY SCHÄFFER FONDS (V527/PS I – 355)

38. LAKE LOUISE IN WINTER

Winter comes early to this wonderful place. The snowfall is extremely heavy and all life seems to cease. Not a bird is heard, scarce even the cry of a coyote. The heavy timbers surrounding the lake prevent the crying of the winter winds, and the only sound to the lonely one is the thunder of an occasional avalanche, which reverberated across the nearby hills.

Lake Louise in Winter

MARY SCHÄFFER FONDS (V527/PS 2 – 38)

39.

Beneath the heavy ice of the lake an occasional hole is cut and some unfortunate fish is caught. So deep is the lake that the better fishing is found at the outlet and even then, they do not seem eager for any bait offered. I am told that the largest fish are caught during the winter.

Lake Louise in Winter

114

40. MT. HUNGABEE, NEAR MORAINE LAKE

A very good motor road has now been established by the government to Moraine Lake from the Chateau [Lake Louise]. So enormous has traffic become that it is called at present "a one way road" as it is too narrow to admit the passing of large cars. The lake is established in the Valley of the Ten Peaks originally known by Stoney Indian numerals. It may be traveled by motor, horse, or on foot. The distance is about nine miles and a dainty lodge is established at the lakeside where one may have a refreshing drink of tea. Approaching the downgrade to the lake is one of the finest sights in the

Mt. Hungabee, the first of the Ten Peaks at Morane [Moraine] Lake, near Lake Louise

MARY SCHÄFFER FONDS
(v527/ps 2 – 40)[92]

116

[Moraine Lake in the Valley of the Ten Peaks]

mountains. The lake has been formed by a huge slide of rock and the waters of many glaciers give it a perfect emerald hue. At one time it was famous as a fishing spot. The mountain in the center of the picture was named by the discoverer of Mt. Hungabee [Chieftain] and is further to the right and is the end of the ten peaks. Mt. Deltaform is further to the right and although it has been climbed it will not be conquered often, as it is considered one of the most difficult peaks in the Rockies.

41.

Lake O'Hara, previously mentioned as a good walking trip from Lake Louise, may be reached very comfortably from Hector Station a few miles west of Lake Louise. It is taken on ponies and is through beautiful country. At present a small chalet stands there and one may enjoy more than the comforts of a tent, [though] personally tent life has no horrors and many things which make it attractive. The lake is about one mile long but is surrounded by magnificent scenery. In this picture, you may see the ice over which an aspiring climber would come from Louise, but the shower of falls from the glaciers behind are not visible.

Lake O'Hara

LONSDALE FONDS (v368/ps 2 – 135)*

42. DRYAS OCTOPETALA

As for the semi-alpine flowers, their numbers and names are legion. When the botanist has finished at Louise he may go and dally at O'Hara where he finds those plants which need a colder climate. The Dryas octopetala is found in the dried river beds going into [these] mountain-locked lakes.

Dryas octopetala

MARY SCHÄFFER FONDS
(V527/PS 2 – 42)

43. BEFORE THE CAMP FIRE

To one accustomed to camping there is something lost when the tiny cabins come stealing into their haunts. Camp life is fascinating. There is never any house-cleaning. When your carpet of flowers wears out, move on, and Nature gets the place in shape for another year. Clothes must be comfortable but very plain. Camp is a place to wash up, to darn up, to sew on buttons, and above all to talk over the thrilling things of the day. It's lovely to tell a tenderfoot how you hit a grouse with a stone at 20 feet when you really knocked the silly bird off a limb at about 5 ft.; to tell him how you caught a big fish with pieces of red flannel – though that is no fib but not very sporty. As for the meals, they sound prosy and rather distasteful but get a good appetite behind them and everything goes.

One of our summer homes (1906)
[Mollie Adams, Mary Schäffer,
William Warren and
Joe Barker in camp]

MARY SCHÄFFER FONDS (DAMAGED) (V439/PS – I)*

44. DR. P.A. COLEMAN

Dr. Coleman, the famous geologist, deserves a place among these pictures. He has been a pioneer to the head waters of the rivers which flow into the Bow, as well as into many other places. His writings are well worth study and some of us had the honour to follow the blazes of his trail into new land. Occasionally we have had the comfort of running into a hunter's cabin and tho' we have always preferred the fresh breezes of our own tepees, one can imagine what those cabins have meant to the trapper in the dead of winter when he may close his door on the cruel winds and snow and build a huge fire of spruce.

[Dr. A.P. Coleman] [1907]

MOORE FAMILY FONDS (V439/PS – 20)*

45 [AND 46. JOINED TOGETHER]
PEAKS AT LAKE O'HARA

At Lake O'Hara there are many excellent mountains for the climber on which to use his skill, among them the Wiwaxy Peaks at the outlet of the lake, Mount Hungabee to the south, Mount Schäffer in the foreground and Mount Odaray in the west. A comfortable walk to Lake McArthur is well worth the slight exertion involved, although I think horses will go there now. It leads gently up to alpine regions where new flowers tempt the botanist. McArthur's altitude is so great that the little lake is seldom free of ice as this photo taken in midsummer shows. Its outlet is at one end of the lake where a most mysterious gurgling goes on constantly as it makes its way in unseen ways beneath the mountain valleys.

Top right: Peaks at Lake O'Hara

MARY SCHÄFFER FONDS (V527/PS 2 – 45)

Right: Peaks at Lake O'Hara

MARY SCHÄFFER FONDS (DAMAGED) (V527/PS 2 – 46)

47.

Swinging the camera round to the left, Mt. Hungabee comes into view. The group of climbers are members of the Alpine Club of Canada, standing about the swirling outlet of the lake, their eyes on great Hungabee, a mountain whose climb would put a feather in anyone's cap.

Lake MacArthur [McArthur], near Lake Louise, an alpine lake far above timberline. Covered with ice, save for a very short time in the summer.

MARY SCHÄFFER FONDS,
PHOTOGRAPHER BYRON HARMON
(DAMAGED) (V527/PS 2 – 47)

48. [AND 49. JOINED TOGETHER] FISHING AT O'HARA

At the time our party visited O'Hara there was no neat cabin but a comfy tent. And while most of us visited the alpine lake of McArthur, the cook was catching a fine string of fish which tasted pretty good at supper time broiled over wood coals. He has also been able to bowl over a "fool-hen," a most aptly named creature. When it sees a human coming it sits still in its tracks or wherever it may be and allows the most unskilled marksman to bring it down with a .22 or a stone. Nothing but the desire for a good supper ever impels the camper to kill a "fool hen." Probably the fact that it sits so perfectly still has saved many a life, as they are almost the color of the surrounding logs and trees. And it often takes a sharp eye to detect the bird.

Grouse, commonly called "fool-hen," native of Rocky Mountains

MARY SCHÄFFER FONDS, PHOTOGRAPHER BYRON HARMON (V527/PS 2 – 49)

Fishing at [Lake] O'Hara

MARY SCHÄFFER FONDS (V527/PS 2 – 48)

50.

The trail back to the railroad from Lake O'Hara is full of interest. The willows in the long stretches of meadow are full of brightness and color. The mosses in the forest are a foot thick and the falls at the end of the ride would be very wonderful if one had not seen so much previously.

Trail from Lake O'Hara

MARY SCHÄFFER FONDS (V527/PS 2 – 50)

124

51. TAKAKAW [TAKAKKAW] FALLS

The station at Field on the CPR affords a splendid starting point for the Yoho Valley. It seems no time since the valley was discovered by a trapper and named by that famous man Sir William Van Horne. The writer was there before cabins or camps were known. The party took horses at Field and made their way to Emerald Lake by the western route. There were 16 people in that marvelous cavalcade who mostly knew no more about horses than the average person does about camels. They camped at the upper end of the lake and from there walked to "Look-off" where they saw for the first time the great falls later known as Takakaw [Takakkaw]. Today a charming little hotel stands above the green lake; at the great falls are cabins and through that part of the park are now innumerable trails where one may see most with minimum fatigue.

Takaka [Takakkaw] Falls in
Yoho National Park, British Columbia

MARY SCHÄFFER FONDS, PHOTOGRAPHER BYRON HARMON
(V527/PS 2 – 51)

52. LAUGHING FALLS

Good trails lead from one waterfall to another and several days may be spent in the valley, as the camps are now of the best. This photo of Laughing Falls fails to give any idea of its natural beauty as the camera has its limitations no matter what the subject.

Laughing Falls

MOORE FAMILY FONDS
PHOTOGRAPHER BYRON HARMON
V439/PS – 197*

53. LAUGHING FALLS IN WINTER

Here it is shown in the grip of winter.
This is perhaps a wonderful time to
behold all nature of the hills asleep,
but few are able to reach those ice-
bound places.

Laughing Falls in Winter

MARY SCHÄFFER FONDS,
PHOTOGRAPHER BYRON HARMON
(V527/PS 2 – 53)

54. TWIN FALLS

The Twin Falls are the most undepend-able of the Yoho Falls. You may take all kinds of trouble to see them and find them one solid mass, again they take their proper name of "Twins." But all depends on the amount of debris which is tossed down the mountains by the spring freshets where at the point of plunging the great precipice a huge boulder is as apt to embed itself as not. But they are beautiful whether showing a single form or double.

Far left: Twin Falls

MARY SCHÄFFER FONDS
(v527/ps 2 – 54)

Left: Twin Falls

MARY SCHÄFFER FONDS
(v527/ps 1 – 372)*

55. GREAT GLACIER AT GLACIER, B.C.

The next most interesting place to visit while on the CPR is the station at Glacier. It was formerly used as an eating house for the tourist and perhaps the scenery was only a secondary consideration but it is there just the same. Before the Connaught Tunnel was placed through the Rogers Pass, thus eliminating the dangers from steep grades and snow-slides in winter, the traveler was greeted by the above sight on reaching the hotel. At present he who wishes to know Glacier better, gets off at the western end of the tunnel and is driven up to Glacier about one and one-half miles. Tell what they may, the snout of the Glacier is but a mile from the hotel. Many fine trails lead to higher points where a horse may go.

Glacier House in winter with Great Glacier in distance

56. IN THE SELKIRKS

Climbing in the Selkirks is markedly different from that in the more eastern Rockies. In the latter a horse may go anywhere, but in the former, owing to the thick undergrowth, you have the pleasure of being your own horse. A few huts have been built at more popular points where a benighted and weary climber may find a sort of rest among mountain rats and squirrels. But there are no spring beds. This photo was taken by a party who wished to see the sun rise from the Hermit Range. They retired amidst brilliant stars, quite visible through the noise, someone said: "Rats," and let it go at that. In the morning they found they had been deluged with soft snow which had slipped and slid down the old roof, in some places alighting on the sleepers, but all admitted they would not have missed the "fairy land" which was theirs for an hour.

[No image matching this description could be found among Mary's slides.]

57. MOUNT MCDONALD [MACDONALD]

So enthusiastic were our photographers that many photos were taken, among them "Mount McDonald" [Macdonald] from the hut. The misty clouds are seen rising from the warm sun beating into the valley below. The walk later in the valley and thence to the hotel was accompanied with many a snow bath and drenched garments, but no one was sorry he went.

Mount McDonald [Macdonald]

MARY SCHÄFFER FONDS,
PHOTOGRAPHER BYRON HARMON
(V527/PS 2 – 57)

58. THE PORCUPINE

So few are the human beings who scale the heights of the Hermit Range that wild life over there is anything but wild. Bears look at the passerby and pay not the slightest attention – unless accompanied by cubs – and the porcupine is always a gentle little creature. He is bound to be feared by the camper as he eats anything from bacon to shoe-strings, and his spines, which have a way of getting loose and falling out, are painful to encounter, but he never seeks trouble. He has a small whimper like a very young child, and woe betide the dog who thinks he can rend or harm the humble porcupine.

Porcupine sunning himself on a tree-stump

MARY SCHÄFFER FONDS,
PHOTOGRAPHER BYRON HARMON
(V527/PS 2 – 58)

132

59. TAMED ANIMALS

Near Glacier are some interesting caves, now called Nakimu. But why I do not know. They were discovered by a hunter by the name of Deutschmann and went by his name for a long time. He was in the Cougar valley hunting bear. After killing a huge grizzly he stopped to investigate a small hole which he saw nearby. He found the place honeycombed with such, and a large stream passed through these holes. With the assistance of the government he materially developed them and eventually was given control of them for the benefit of sightseers. He had everything in sight trained to come to him. He had built himself a small shack, fed his gophers and marmots and squirrels, and even went so far as to show us a tame fly. Whether he ever made pets of the grizzlies which were around his place in numbers I do not know. At least he never allowed the stranger to travel about unaccompanied. Here are two of his pets who care no more for the watching tourist than the tree behind them. But he always seemed to have an eye out for the advancing grizzly coming up the flower-swept slopes.

Tamed animals

MARY SCHÄFFER FONDS
(DAMAGED) (V527/PS 2 – 59)

60. SKIING IN THE SELKIRKS

Skis and snow-shoes are the best form of getting about in the Selkirks, where the fall of snow is greater than in any other part of Canada. From 40 to 60 inches have been reported in one season, and it is not hard to believe, as measuring snow is about all one has to do when acting as caretaker of that place. The fall of the feathery flakes seems incessant till spring comes, when the rain takes its place, and goes on with the game. The climate is much more moist than that of the Rockies and consequently the flora is different.

Skeeing [Skiing] at Glacier, B.C.

MARY SCHÄFFER FONDS
(v527/ps 2 – 60)

51. SNOW MUSHROOMS

Having no summer flowers handy I have placed here the winter "mushrooms," the old stumps of trees which grow more and more loaded with the softly falling snow, and as there is almost no wind they hold till spring with its drenching showers.

Below: Snow mushrooms, Glacier, B.C.

MARY SCHÄFFER FONDS (DAMAGED) (V527/PS 2 – 61)

Above: Snow mushroom

MARY SCHÄFFER FONDS (DAMAGED) (V527/PS 2 – 61A)

I have run hurriedly and sketchily through these slides, but they were never intended originally to see the light of day beyond the hospitals of England during the war. It might be of interest to some of my listeners that more than one poor lad from Alberta recognized something from HOME. I received one letter in which the writer said, "I had a splendid night last night. Was wheeled into the assembly hall of the hospital and there were the photos of Banff; it was dark enough that the other fellows did not see the tears. It made me pretty homesick, but I am getting along alright and will soon be back." Never having thought of them as instructive to others, it was not till the slides returned to Edmonton that it was suggested that they might be put in form for others who had not had the chance of beholding their own country and especially that part of it which surpasses all other countries the writer has ever visited. Thus I have collected a second series of the mountains which portray quite a different section, but as the listeners might weary, although I feel sure their pride in their country could never wane, I have classified them under the head of: At the Head Waters of the Saskatchewan and Athabaska Rivers.

IN THE HEART OF THE CANADIAN ROCKIES, PART II

At the Head Waters of the Saskatchewan and Athabaska [Athabasca]:
A Sequel to "In the Heart of the Canadian Rockies"
by Mary S. Warren, Banff, Alberta

Lest one's hearers weary of what in a day's play to those who have made the many tiring but delightful marches into almost unknown country, our last talk finished with one summer's work, only to find us eager to go yet farther afield the next year. All winter long we had been tasting all the dried vegetables and things which would lighten the loads of our faithful friends, the horses. Our minds were on a lake said by the Stoney Indians to be about 300 miles north of Louise, although I think as the crow flies it will be found very much shorter. However, it was a good excuse to be in the open, to follow the trail for the simple love of following it, and explore places of which we knew nothing. Very few men, save trappers, had gone far to the north, and no women had felt they had any particular business that way. We searched for maps and found none, but why bother about maps when there were sun, stars, rivers, and plenty of food we meant to take.

One of our party was blessed with plenty of brains for the lot of us, so we went in spite of all the fatalities which kindly imaginations were willing to deal out to us. It is a number of years

Outfit of 1908

MARY SCHÄFFER FONDS (V527/PS I – 55)*

now since we took that trip. We have never been
sorry and only wonder that more have not done
the same. It is a well-known route now and we
managed to make a map which has been of considerable value to others since. It is one of the finest
trips in the mountains.

[Camp in burnt timber][93]

MARY SCHÄFFER FONDS (V527/PS I – 155)*

1. [AND 2. JOINED TOGETHER]

The upper Bow Valley is very picturesque with fine lakes, rivers and mountains. This little snap was taken from the back of a horse at Bow Lake. The shores are all muskeg so the best footing is in the water. On the shores of the lake and over the Bow Pass the flowers grow in great profusion. These photos of the Dryas drummondii and the Cassiope mertensiana (false heather) are of two of the more common species. The false heather is a carpet of glory in the hills, and strange to say, the passing of a bunch of horses never seems to do the slightest harm to the wonderful flower garden.

Above: Dryas drummondii, Field – 6.7:05

MARY SCHÄFFER FONDS
(V527/PS 3 – 2)

Below: Trail on Bow Lake

MARY SCHÄFFER FONDS (V527/PS 3 – 1)

Left: Cassiope mertensiana – Heather

MARY SCHÄFFER FONDS
(V527/PS 3 – 2A)

3.

At the upper end of the lake our small panoramic camera recorded for our homesick minds the last familiar mountains; all that we were venturing towards would be strangers to us. It is impossible to give the trip entire, but just a snatch here and there may give some idea of that vast country of hills.

[Mountains and Lakes]

MARY SCHÄFFER FONDS (V439/PS – 87)

4.

Slowly making our way up the North Saskatchewan we turned into a side valley known as the "West Branch of the North Fork of the Saskatchewan." This was an almost untouched bit of country, just a trapper and one explorer of whom we knew had taken a glimpse of it. It was quite a long trend, but one worthwhile. We knew of Mt. Bryce in this section, and also Mt. Alexandra, as well as some ice fields. Our camp was established under the shadow of Watchman's Peak. The following morning we made a partial ascent, reaching a shoulder of Mt. Bryce. A year or so later the writer had the honor of showing this beautiful mountain to England's Ambassador to the United States, Mr. Bryce, at one of the American Geographical Societies. It was his first view of it, and he received firsthand the history of the scramble we had made on the scree slopes of his namesake, in our desire to see the great ice fields of Mount Columbia, which Sir James Outram has proclaimed the largest outside the Arctic Circle. We found them, but it was so bitterly cold we were glad to take the photo and then slip down to Thompson Pass, which looked both into Bush Valley in the west and our temporary home in the valley below, and where we could see plainly the smoke of our camp-fire.

Mt. Bryce

MARY SCHÄFFER FONDS (V527/PS 3 – 4)

5.

Mount Coleman was named for one of the pioneers of these two rivers of the north. He was the first man to attempt the ascent of Mt. Robson, the highest peak in the Rockies. That he failed was not to be wondered, but he left his knowledge for others and they profited by it. Dr. Coleman is Geographer, Scientist and Explorer, a man of whom Canada may well be proud.

[Mount Coleman]

MARY SCHÄFFER FONDS (V527/PS 3 – 5)

6.

This shows the first effort of the novice to cross a large and turbulent river – the Saskatchewan. We were well frightened at least two days before, as a sudden thaw had set in, but when the crucial moment came, scenery, mountains, everything fell into the background, for one idea had entered my head: I was wondering how the sugar supply was going to stand such a wetting. For the time being it was quite safe, though later, not having waterproof bags, it shrank so perceptibly that we arrived at the stage where a cake tasted good with just dried fruits in it. Having made our crossing in safety, even the sugar was forgotten as we sat on the high sandy banks and studied the wonderful country all about us. At this particular point the panorama of the mountains is perhaps the finest in the Rockies.

[Mary Schäffer crossing the Saskatchewan River]

MARY SCHÄFFER FONDS (v527/ps 3 – 6)

7.

Here at this point the Saskatchewan is in its infancy. Well, I never want to cross it when it reaches manhood. It wanders in its vastness among the sand-dunes which are largely covered as the river rises higher and higher with the summer sun on the snow fields not five miles away. It is a treacherous river as are all mountain rivers, whose sand bars are here today and gone to another point tomorrow. Swimming is also an art. I think a cool head and a good horse are the greatest essentials for crossing. The writer did not have the first, just a pretence, but was possessed of a horse which knew no fear in the water. And we did not come to grief though we had many chances to do so.

[Saskatchewan River]

MARY SCHÄFFER FONDS (v527/ps 3 – 7)

144

8.

Though we had crossed the river bathed in sunshine, there is no accounting for what may come along the next day. One day the flowers and bees and butterflies make the miles of travel a delight, then comes a snowstorm out of nowhere and those who must make so many miles a day to be sure of a destination, are forced to don slickers and are well equipped with a certain amount of self pity as the cold flakes settle down the back or leave wet bushes through which to drag wet legs, and the laden horses come in for a goodly share of sympathy as their heavy packs gather pounds of wet snow. For the whole cavalcade must keep straight ahead till good horse feed is in sight, no matter where it is found, in burnt timber or soft ground. Horses are the first and last to be considered at all.

[Unknown mountain]

MARY SCHÄFFER FONDS (V527/PS 3 – 8)

9. [AND 10. JOINED TOGETHER]

This shows a little glimpse of rock and water beside the dim trail on the ascent to the Wilcox Pass. It's not a nice pass, but it is full of weariness and you may not jump from your horse to take neat little snapshots, for your horse would walk on quite regardless of your absence and you can never pick up for want of breath, as the pass is exceptionally high. Mt. Athabaska shows wonderfully from the first summit of the pass and at its base is a beautiful ice grotto or cave. Running down to it [the ice cave] one day, we found the coloring magnificent, and all about it were the footprints of wild animals. Alas, the coming of our big outfit had scared away all game and we only knew of their presence by the number of little footmarks in the soft earth. We did behold a beautiful cross fox there one day, but the one and only rifle had come to a useless end by having its front sight knocked off.

Right: [Ascent to Wilcox Pass]

MARY SCHÄFFER FONDS
(V527/PS 3 – 9)

Below: [Mount Athabasca ice grotto or cave]

MARY SCHÄFFER FONDS
(V527/PS 3 – 10)

II.

The trend of the Wilcox Pass is long and tedious, much soft earth to be encountered and a general never-endingness about it. A few hundred feet down the north side is found an old camp known as Sheep Camp. The first time we went that way, we followed our noses and stumbled down what we chose to call "Tangle Creek." It is far from interesting, being excessively steep, but he who goes now, must look to the left and will find a most delightful trail which will lead him comfortably to the Sun Wapta, which is a branch of the Athabaska. He crosses Sheep Creek to find this old trail.

Sun Wapta [Sunwapta River]
branch of R. Atha [Athabasca River]

MARY SCHÄFFER FONDS (V527/PS 3 – II)

12.

The Sun Wapta has its rise in the moist meadows below Wilcox Pass, but is yet too steep to take horses over. There are any number of falls, but they are quite unphotographical, they are within a very short distance of the junction of this small river with the main Athabaska. We had been told to look for a "bridge." Behold it. Our men traversed it and reported it not only safe, but a fine photo was taken from its center. We grabbed up the camera and went to look for this place of "Safety." One look was enough. By getting the second member of our small group to take hold of the only piece of garment which seemed holdable, we crawled as near the rough-hewn log with all its limbs waiting to catch anything catchable, and snapped — and it's about all it is — a snap. But not the finest bit of scenery would ever have taken me on that old, disreputable log, on one end of which was scribbled: "No toll."

[Log "bridge" over Sunwapta River]

MARY SCHÄFFER FONDS (V527/PS 3 – 12)

13.

Many fires have swept the south shores of the Athabaska, and for a few miles it was very hard on the laden horses. Flies were VERY bad – flies, meaning bull-dogs, deerflies, horse flies, and millions of mosquitoes. There was no map of the country, but no one could mistake the Athabaska swirling by. We did not even feel elated – that came later – it was imperative to get a photo of the first glimpse of that great river, and how we got it I am not sure. Someone waved a branch of balsam over the operator, who had doubts that the lens would be so clouded with insects that nothing would come of her attempt. But it is astonishing what a cheap camera will do under stress of circumstances.

Athabaska [Athabasca] River

MARY SCHÄFFER FONDS (V527/PS 3 – 13)

14.

It seemed proper to find a trail leading down the south side of the river, but nothing of that sort being available, the outfit decided to cross and look for one on the north side. There proved to [be] none on the north side either, but all was going well till "Dandy" a great favorite fell into the water. That water was cool, it stopped the flies from biting, and Dandy decided to continue to float. His blankets acted as life preservers and he had not had such a good time for many a long day. All the coaxing in the world would not bring him back to his pals and when at last he was ready to follow the bunch, the land was not there for him to climb to. It had all been undermined by the current. It looked like the loss of one of our best horses, and the animal showed signs of being weary and frightened. The river was running very high and swift, so Dandy did the only thing he could — swam for a solid sand-bar. There he stood. It meant a wetting for the rescuer, but after two hours he was taken upstream and landed safely once again among his friends. In the meantime those who could do nothing in the predicament, were watching the scenery, and observed a snowy pyramidal mountain in the distance.

It is very indistinct in the photo, but as we seemed to have come to the end of our tether in finding a mythical lake, we thought that unknown peak looked very tempting.

[Mount Columbia]

MARY SCHÄFFER FONDS (V527/PS I – 323)*

15.

We made camp. Dandy's allowance of sugar had shrunk violently, through his pleasant swim, the blankets had to be all stretched out to get some of the Athabaska out of them and after a good supper we all turned in for a good night's sleep. The tap-tap of the tin washbasin told us next morning that all would soon be "set" for the unknown pyramid. Through reading the papers of Jean Habel and Dr. Coleman, we had a vague idea of where things in general were. But a delicious uncertainty enveloped the day's work. We doubled back on our tracks and found Chaba Imne, a small stream which flows from Fortress Lake, a lake which is the backbone of the whole range of peaks. Turning south at Chaba Imne, and the river which comes from the Columbia Valley, we found ourselves in a most beautiful but rather difficult valley which led direct to Mt. Columbia itself.

On the Chaba [River]

MARY SCHÄFFER FONDS (V527/PS 3 – 15)

16.

This mountain forms a perfect pyramid on the north side while on its south side are the great ice fields which Outram describes so glowingly. We dragged our weary horses to the verge of the mountain and found no feed whatever, so were forced to take them back several miles to two small islands which had little enough on them but enough to suffice for a couple of days. It had doubtless been a great hunting ground for the Crees of the north. Bones were found aplenty. Cree writing on the trees and even the fresh tracks of caribou in the wet sands. A toad was the solitary thing of live we saw, and that was in my bed. But we had a wonderful time photographing Columbia from her most stately point of vantage. This mountain was first climbed from the south face by Sir James Outram. We had no aspirations for the north side. It is still available for someone else.

Mt. Columbia

MARY SCHÄFFER FONDS (V527/PS 3 – 16)

17.

Returning to Chaba Imne, we made a side trip to Fortress Lake, discovered I think by Dr. Coleman. The name itself was suggested by a fortress-like mountain lying east of the lake itself. It has two outlets, one to the east and one to the west. The camping should be established well away from the lake, as it is very marshy. Great owls hooted to us all night as we lay in our oozing beds, and we were glad to leave the next day. The timber about there is remarkably fine but the underbrush is hopeless. Within a short distance of the lakes is a group of peaks which I think Jean Habel named the Black Friars. Very apt is the name, whoever did it.

Black Friars at Fortress Lake

18.

The year we visited Fortress Lake ended without finding the most indefinitely described lake which we had really gone to search. The fall snows would soon be coming down on the passes, food would be giving out, and as one summer is sure to follow another we were forced to return to civilization. Returning home via the Saskatchewan Plains we were lucky in getting an odd sketch map from an Indian [Sampson Beaver] who had seen the lake in his boyhood and which he called Chaba Imne, or Beaver Lake. With this map, a number more horses and more food we were ready for a whole summer's campaign. By this time the country was well known to us till Brazeau Lake was passed.

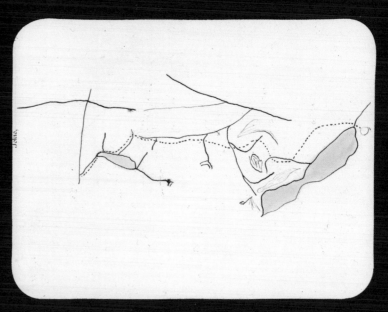

Above: [Sampson's map, 1908]

MARY SCHÄFFER FONDS
(v527/ps 1 – 53)*

Opposite: Sampson Beaver's family, 1906

MARY SCHÄFFER FONDS
(v527/ps 1 – 5)*

19.

Crossing Brazeau Lake at its outlet, all was new and very uncertain, as Indians are not specially trained in map making. The day's march was naturally much shorter, as each mile and each valley was scanned to see if we might by chance be on the right road. We did find cuttings which we thought might have been made by that intrepid explorer Dr. Coleman, and great would be the excitement when we saw a notch in a tree. Great conclaves took place at the campfire. After two days march, climbing any old hill which looked as though it might disclose something ahead we came upon this pass which was eventually named Maligne Pass. But that was long after we had learned we were steadily going toward our goal. It was an attractive pass, quite high, covered with patches of snow, plenty of astonished ptarmigan and surrounded with high peaks.

Maligne Pass

MARY SCHÄFFER FONDS
(V527/PS 3 – 19)

20.

As our longing eyes traveled down far slopes, even our scenic filled minds had to admit it was one of the fairest valleys we had ever beheld. There was not the first sign that fire had ever visited that section, which is uncommon, and the flowers veritably carpeted our way for miles. To our joy, about halfway down, we saw old tepee poles standing, which at least denoted that the way was passable, and that in the past Indians had been up the valley. A fine campground was discovered and from it one of our party made a high climb, returning the soul of weariness, but able to gasp between mouthfuls of hot bacon and bannock that he had located the lake, which was not eight miles distant. We even forgot the mosquitoes in our excitement and it was well after midnight before the camp settled to rest.

[Teepee Poles]

MARY SCHÄFFER FONDS
(V527/PS I – 76)

21.

After reaching the lake all hands wondered where the horses were to find feed, for it looked a fairly sizable lake. Just as we crossed a large stream looking for permanent feed[,] Old Buck lost a whole bag of flour. It fell not two ft. from the water, which is one of the nice accidents to record, for it could so easily be rescued. A most perfect pasture was found for the large number of horses, such a one that they did not have the slightest desire to roam. Mosquitoes were in profusion and while the men were lashing a sort of raft together, the feminine element was making "bug nets" for the family. The third day saw the party toting tents, food, wraps and the dog aboard, and there was far more excitement than even a trip to Europe would cause. Why not? This was perhaps the first craft to ever sail the new lake.

Rafting Maligne Lake, 1908

MARY
SCHÄFFER
FONDS
(V527/PS 3 – 21)

22.

Such work as that great log-made raft took to drive it through the silent waters no one knows save those who did the work. As we slowly approached the double-headed peak here shown, Mr. Unwin, one of our co-workers, suddenly exclaimed: "That is the peak from which I first saw the lake!" In jest someone said: "Let's name it for him." The name is there today, a beautiful monument to one of the finest men of Banff who gave his life in the Great War. It is thus lightly we place names on the monarchs of the hills but this one will never slightly be borne. The second peak bears the name of a man who helped us materially to accomplish our work. It is called Mt. Charlton, named for Mr. H.R. Charlton of the Grand Trunk Pacific. Later, when the G.T.P. had made its way through the Yellowhead Pass, Mr. Charlton was one of the first men to realize that this lake was going to be one of the great scenic points of the country about Jasper, and time has proved it. He aided very materially the survey of the lake in conjunction with our park authority Mr. Howard Douglas, and after many trials the lake was shown to be 18 miles long.

Mounts Charlton and Unwin from lower end of Maligne Lake

MARY SCHÄFFER FONDS (V527/PS 3 – 22)

23.

It took two days to row that cumbersome raft to the upper part of the lake, and back. Had not enthusiasm run so high, I think our torn and bleeding hands would have made us turn back. But all stuck to the work and found the upper part of the lake a gem indeed. Waterfalls are there in plenty, an occasional avalanche thundered down some hidden ravine, and the glaciers reflected themselves in a mirror of the stillest water. No one wanted to leave the wonderful place, but we knew we must get back to the horses, to make our way round to the lower end of the lake and get down to the Athabaska according to our Indian map.

On Lake Maligne

MARY SCHÄFFER FONDS
(V527/PS 3 – 23)

24.

Paddling the ungainly craft down the lake in the evening, the sun fell behind the hills, and over the higher peaks came the most wonderful alpine glow. Above us frowned a peak which was specially brilliant and it was suggested to name it for the Indian who had given us the rather sketchy map. As it lay closely to the narrows which the man had drawn for us, we just naturally named it Sampson's Peak and Sampson's Narrows. We mistook them for main land till we found a winding way among the hills. They are perhaps the most picturesque part of the whole lake.

[Sampson's Peak]

MARY SCHÄFFER FONDS (V527/PS 3 – 24)

25.

The following day our horses reluctantly left their haven of natural feed and we made our way easily to the lower end of the lake. Here we came near having the only real catastrophe that we ever encountered in the many miles of the several years we followed the trail. On the opposite side of the outlet of the lake, our best shot saw goat in any number roving the hills. He decided on a good steak for supper. Seeing a perfectly marked trail leading down to the outlet and coming out on the other side, he prepared for his very short swim. All of us were watching him and were astounded at his horse suddenly rising on end and then tumbling over backward. They both swam back to shore and the hunter perhaps made some rather impolite remarks to his horse for failing him so badly. They both had been upset. Another strong horse was chosen and the same performance took place. By this time it was beaten in on our brains that

though that outlet looked as still as a pond, there was a terrible undertow which bowled over any horse that tried to swim it. The Indians had probably done their swimming late in the fall when the water was much less powerful. Needless to say we went without goat that night. This picture was taken the next day a little further up stream, and all went well.

Getting our second horse back on the side where we were all camped was no joke. He was a favorite. He stood quite still after his troubles in the water and the men rushed to put any sort of raft together to reach him. It was a most trying time. All the other horses took the occasion to try and get back to their feeding place of two days ago. The writer had to run about three miles in muskeg to get them headed back. On reaching camp again, the raft was still in progress and the other useless member of camp was putting out the various garments of the ex-hunter to dry. In our outfit was one beautiful young horse which they said still had a few teeth to cut. The laundry seemed of every hue imaginable and tired as I was it looked funny till I suddenly beheld Baldy (he of the new teeth) suddenly take from the improvised clothesline a shirt which was the color of a canary. Whether it was the color which attracted him or what I do not know, but as he sallied off and I was the only one who saw his theft, and shirts were none too numerous, I could have shed honest tears as I went galloping after him in my wet moccasins. It was a mile's chase and when reached, Baldy must have been chewing all the time, for the whole sleeve was down his throat, and as it was pulled up, it was full of holes. Such is trail life.

Crossing at mouth of Maligne [Lake]

MARY SCHÄFFER FONDS (DAMAGED) (V527/PS 3 – 25)

On the return of our half-drowned Dandy, the family settled down for the night and not even to this day do they know who was the heroine. She had to be sorry all by herself. The following day it was decided to use the improvised raft to swim the horses over to the other side of the outlet, as feed was fine and horses could be held there indefinitely.

Crossing the Mouth of Maligne [1908]

MARY SCHÄFFER FONDS (V527/PS 3 – 26)

27.

It was a hard day's moving. Everyone was tired and everyone wanted a complete rest and even before tents were put up or the inevitable tea prepared, they RESTED.

Lower end of Maligne Lake

MARY SCHÄFFER FONDS (V527/PS 3 – 27)

Knowing by a sort of instinct now that this river of the big lake must be the river known by hunters for years as Maligne River, which falls into Athabaska River, we gave the lake the name which some Frenchmen of years ago must have left behind, and now the lake is known as the Maligne. Pretty apt it seemed to me after nearly losing one man and two good horses at its very start. From here we fully intended to make our way down the Maligne River, only a matter of 35 miles, to the Athabaska, but it's easier to plan than to succeed. While the players played at laundry, at cooking impossible dishes out of impossible things, and sewing on buttons with shoe thread, the workers were trying to surmount the insurmountable. The numbers of fires had thrown a network of trees over the entire valley. Nothing larger than a rat could have gone through that fallen timber, and at last we were forced to go round 100 miles to reach the river of olden days we so longed to see.

Above: [Camp at Maligne Lake, 1908]

MARY SCHÄFFER FONDS (V527/PS I – 69)*

Right: A hard bit in the bush

MARY SCHÄFFER FONDS (V527/PS I – 17)*

29.

One morning we sadly packed up, took a last photo of the friendly hills and started on the long detour which we knew to be ahead. It's very hard
to be balked thus when one has gone through so
much. Referring to the name given the lake, I will
say here there has been a good deal of criticism.
But having been upheld by the Royal Geographical
Society, I may give the reason for so unfortunate a name. Opposite the old North-West Fur
Trading House, known as Henry House, the Maligne
River runs into the Athabaska, and that last ar-
biter of Geographical Commendation or censure
says one name must be retained as much as possible. So there are at present Maligne Lake, River, Pass,
Mountain and Valley. Easy to remember, not easy
to forget once seen.

Lake Maligne fr. [from] the summit of Mount Unwin, 1908

MARY SCHÄFFER FONDS, PHOTOGRAPHER
SID UNWIN (v527/ps 1 – 61)*

30.

This photo and the one following are almost a panorama. After several days of steady travel over unknown ground, we saw the valley of the Athabaska. Trails led in all directions and ended nowhere. Fires had swept in every direction and nothing eliminates a trail like a fire. The afternoon this photo was taken, two of us stood on a high hill overlooking what is now known to be the Miette Valley. The horses had borrowed all our own discouragement and scarce took the trouble to swish a tail at an occasional fly. The men had gone off to look for somewhere or something which would give us a clew [clue] of advancement. We had nothing to say – just stood. Imagine the enchantment of the sound of a rifle on the far side of the river where was previously nothing but soundlessness. We had nothing to signal back. We and the horses were standing on the skyline and something human had seen us. Of course we waved our hands and yelled but the shot was easily five miles away. Later we learned that an Indian who had his whole family out on the fall hunt had seen us and thinking it was some pal who was looking for him had sent the shot. No one can guess our thrill who had not seen another human being but ourselves for months.

168

Looking down the Athabaska [Athabasca] near Mt. Hardisty [1908]

31.

Our man returned with the information that we could get a good camp-site within a few yards but the land must be studied as to further advance. Our desire was to cross the Athabaska, see Mt. Robson and behold the Tête Jaune Cache, all mentioned in the old history of the country. The river at that point was impossible, and a band of earth at least 30 ft. high demanded a detour. We were getting rather sick of detours. The following morning, after passing a wasp's nest on a steep slope, we all landed up against the tall bank to see what was to happen. The least valuable horses were tried first and it was a marvel of patience and skill that the whole bunch was put over eventually without one accident. Today at the place where we had to drop down with such caution is a series of bridges across the great river, and few people really believe that 32 horses went over this particular spot in safety. Finding a camping place, we very soon learned the significance of the word "maligne." There was no such thing as crossing that river at its entrance to the larger river. It is probably possible in late fall, but not when we were there.

169

At Maligne Gorge

MARY SCHÄFFER FONDS (V527/PS 3 – 31)

32.

After a night's rest we started up the west side of the river, and soon located horse-tracks – more excitement—but all great days on the trail are made up of small things. The river was soon hemmed in by rocks, and then a gorge of fine dimensions began to appear. The horse-trail led beside this wild and more wild gorge. One sat [on] one's horse and gazed down into utter darkness and the roaring of an unseen river. You who go our way today will never know the thrill of that ride. They have built a motor road and of course motor roads are not clinging to dangerous brinks. It made me a wee bit sad the first time I saw the "improvement."

Maligne Gorge

MARY SCHÄFFER FONDS (V527/PS 3 – 32)

33·

As we climbed to the highest point of the gorge we looked back to the Miette River flowing from the north, we knew beyond that was the Yellowhead Pass. Would we ever reach it? It was very tantalizing. The roar of the Maligne grew less and less and as we reached the main river, it was so small one could walk across it with the greatest ease. Later we were to learn that the Maligne coming from the lake flowed into Medicine Lake, which at low water had no surface outlet but allowed the water to trickle underground. Here it followed the underground course till it came to light once again through various channels in the great gorge itself. A very fair trail now leads straight to Maligne Lake and at any time we may hear that the ubiquitous motor car is carrying sight-seers to the lake in so many hours at so much per head. Alas for the Indian pony and the tepee, they will soon be relegated to a museum.

Maligne Gorge – looking toward Miette Valley

MARY SCHÄFFER FONDS (V527/PS 3 – 33)

34.

After circumnavigating the gorge our cavalcade tumbled down
the hill to the river again and gazed and gazed across to the
north shore, wondering: "Where is Swift?" Swift needs some ex-
plaining, or at least he did in those days. We had a fair idea of
general conditions through Dr. McEvoy's report and map along
the Athabaska, and he had mentioned this white man who had
come into the valley to live and to wait for a rail-road to make
its appearance. If we could get hold of Swift we might be able to
get over that wide, wild river. But Swift was not to be seen, nor
any habitation. A little later we could dimly see a shack on the
north side, and at last reached an Indian home – but alas on
the south side. There was no thought of swimming across on the
horses' backs, so they were unpacked, allowed to graze and we
sat down to tea and to think it over. Before eating we fired a rifle
just on general principles. The dug-outs, of which there were
two, bobbed and curtsied in the most tantalizing way from the
other side, and it looked as though our Mt. Robson trip was come
to naught.

[Lewis Swift]

MARY SCHÄFFER FONDS (V527/PS I – 92)*

35.

However, we had learned not to worry, and to take Mr. Micawber's assurance that "something would turn up." While enjoying some fine wild strawberries and condensed cream, a noise was heard and the wildest looking being was seen coming across dancing waters in one of the dug-outs. HE WAS SWIFT! We women were as much a surprise to him as he to us. He was quite sure we were either prospectors or timber cruisers. The fact that we could possibly be out for fun was beyond his imagination. He helped to get the horses into the water and across in great style. How the poor things hated it! We did not stay too near as we felt pretty sure he had a language of his own for getting them there.

173

[Horses crossing Maligne River]

MARY SCHÄFFER FONDS (v527/PS 3 – 35)

36.

When our turn came for going, he lashed two of the dug-outs together, and took us over in pieces, so to speak. Some of the food went with each passenger. I being on the last trip, saw a storm coming but took my place as requested, and as we got into the maelstrom of water felt as though I was riding an almond shell, but arrived in perfect safety. It was rather annoying to find that the swimming horses had all taken to their heels as soon as they got over and also that a real storm was coming. We who had nothing to do with the game, dragged things under a limp tent, made a sickly fire, and had a hot cup of coffee when the men got back from looking up all their lost property. That we had succeeded was the main thing after all.

[Crossing Maligne River]

MARY SCHÄFFER FONDS (V527/PS I – 89)*

We found Swift a remarkable character. He had already been in the country 15 years, sure to the last that a rail-road would come. He had his own grain, his forge, his horses and cattle. He came originally from Buffalo, N.Y., which took him by way of Edmonton. He had brought all his animals from Edmonton over muskeg, which took two weeks. All his shopping was done there and he did not shop often. He knew the railroad was started and said he meant to wait now till he could go to the rails. This photo shows his first little home and family and today a transcontinental train thunders by his door. It has been too much for him, he has moved to a quieter spot.

[Mrs. Lewis Swift and four children in front of their house, 1908]

MARY SCHÄFFER FONDS (V527/PS 1 – 94)

38.

His family numbered about 5. His horses and cows were of the best. He had built his own flour mill, run by water power of course, and had even brought chickens over that terrible trail. He proved most hospitable. After the months of bacon and dried stuff, no one can imagine how good the great jug of milk tasted which he brought us and the fresh eggs and potatoes and cabbages. The two nights our tepees were pitched under one of his big Douglas firs, he would sit in the firelight and tell us of his early days in that country, of his trapping and those days when he drove a stage in the land where hold-ups were common.

Swift's Flour-Mill

MARY SCHÄFFER FONDS (V527/PS 3 – 38)

39.

It was all so thrilling and all a piece of the past and we could have dallied a week but we had far to go if we meant to see Mount Robson and the Cache, and we parted with our hosts with reluctance. The Yellowhead Pass has long been known as the lowest pass across the continent in Canada, and we saw signs of many having gone that way before. On our route we came to this grave of which Swift had told us in his own way. "Yuh see there was a feller who used to bring prospectors in – who had any dough[94] – But somehow they got lost and he never took 'em out again. Then some other feller who heard of his losing so many customers, decided he wasn't going to be lost and he WAS goin' to find the way in. So it ended in the guide being left behind that time." This was supposed to be the villain's grave – I give it as I heard it.

Grave at Grand Fork [Forks]

MARY SCHÄFFER FONDS (V527/PS 3 – 39)

40.

Swift gave us a very vivid description of what we would find in the way of a trail to the west. It far surpassed anything he had said about it. At that time the pegs which denoted the coming of a railroad could be seen here and there. No attempt to construct anything in the line of trail had been done. We had huge fallen timber to hop over, an occasional corpse of some hapless horse to pass. We passed up the Miette Valley which hails from the Yellowhead summit and found it a valley of wonderful fruits of many kinds. It was difficult to make out which mountain was which, but at the time this was taken, we thought it was Mt. Pelee. There was a Mt. Geikie somewhere and since then a lovely mountain has been named, as we all know, for that wonderful woman Edith Cavell. This latter is very near the present site of Jasper. Many were the dishes of great raspberries we had in the valley of the Miette, but one did not care to stray far alone for them as it was all too evident the bears liked them as well as we did.

Looking toward
Yellowhead
Pass Athabaska
[Athabasca] River
Miette Valley [1908]

MARY SCHÄFFER FONDS
(V527/PS 1 – 99)

41.

The actual crossing of the summit of the pass would have gone unnoticed except for the fact that a weary looking tree had been scored a number of times with initials and the fact blazoned thereon that this was Yellowhead Pass. It was most unimpressive and disappointing as a scenic point but must have been a treasure to the engineers who had grades and winter snows to consider. Our minds were now on the highest peak of the Rockies, Mt. Robson. The first record of its height had been established at about 17,000 feet I think, but it has steadily dwindled with each batch of surveyors who went in there. The last I heard of it officially was about 13,008 ft., but some of our listeners may be even better posted than the writer. No matter what its height, it is a noble mountain and well worth the enthusiasm it has created. Clouds have a fashion of descending on views just at the wrong moment, so the first glimpse was not as it should be. Later we had a fine view of the south face, but that negative was broken.

First Glimpse of Mt. Robson [1908]

MOORE FAMILY FONDS (V439/PS 53)*

42.

To add to this series of photos a friend has added a picture of this now famous peak taken on its northern side. The whole north of the mountain is far more scenic than the south, and so many pictures of it have been taken that it seems useless to describe it. As the trans-continental train rushes towards the east from the Pacific Mt. Robson is considered one of the finest sights of the whole road. Traveling over that road a few years ago and trying to locate some of the places where we had had such difficult times finding footing for our horses, I was suddenly surprised and also amused to hear a voice say: "Madam, if you will look straight ahead you will see Mt. Robson, the etc. etc." He meant well, and so I tried to be as surprised and delighted as all the rest of the car was. But in fact I was trying to find a spot where the whole lot of us nearly slid into the Fraser River one fine morning and where we jumped the most awful stumps of old trees, and to find the Cache and a lot of other things which could only interest those who had gone over every inch of the way, in the days when it was a hard saddle and not a plush seat of a very comfortable car.

Top: [Mount Robson, 1908]

MARY SCHÄFFER FONDS (V527/PS I – 104)

Bottom: [Mount Robson, 1909]

MARY SCHÄFFER FONDS (V527/PS I – 322)*

43.

We attempted the south face of Mt. Robson but that is a hopeless proposition owing to the tremendous growth. In a notch of its lower slopes however is a charming lake of the greenest hue, called Lake Helena. The Alpine Club of Canada has taken a great interest in the mountain and its surroundings. It has now been climbed a number of times, but it is always more or less difficult. As I understand it, Moose River is now the route to take to see the best of Robson, but there are plenty of fine guides at present at Jasper who can give complete details. I have written this from the standpoint of a newcomer, and all we could behold was the south face.

Lake Helena [Helena Lake] – Mt. Robson

MARY SCHÄFFER FONDS (DAMAGED) (V527/PS 3 – 43)*

44.

At the time our party visited the Cache, the trail was all that Swift described, with a little more thrown in. There were the merest footholds in instances, where the turn of a foot would have sent rider and horse down into the rushing Fraser River. It was excessively stony in places, very boggy in others. It was dusty in places, but after all we had seen just as bad or worse. Swift had been so very vivid in his description that we were just naturally looking for something fearsome, and doubtless it had been thus for some of those who had gone ahead of us with horses not trained to trail life. Our own horses were so accustomed to making allowances for their packs in tight places, so perfectly capable of looking after their own necks, that we found it not at all bad after all.

A slippery spot on Fraser [1908]

MOORE FAMILY FONDS (V439/PS – 54)

Except for the narrowness of the footing in some parts on the Fraser, the last part of the way to the Cache was perhaps the worst as the stones proved pretty hard on the ponies' feet. Swift's description of the kind of people we might meet on the trail was as flowery as the rest of his descriptions and I think the women of our party looked for nothing short of murderers. Turning the last corner of the trail we beheld this peaceful view. On the other side of the river was a small Indian village with great fruit-drying racks stretched to the bright sun. On our side just one little shack and a tent in the distance. The shack was surrounded by a flimsy fence and against it leaned a man, — nay, two men — unshaven and generally cut-throat in appearance. They looked in silence at our coming, which some of us mistook for hostility; later we found they were too astonished to speak, as we were the first white women they had seen in this district.

Fraser [River] near Tête Jaun [Jaune]

MARY SCHÄFFER FONDS (v527/ps 3 – 45)

46.

We camped in the brush back of their shack and some of us felt rather frightened. It was the usual case of *JUDGING A MAN BY HIS CLOTHES.* In about an hour, he who had looked the villain of the piece, appeared at our tent with a huge salmon freshly caught which he thought "the ladies might enjoy." You would not have known him. The month-old beard had faded away, the old khaki garments had been replaced by a nicely fitting suit. He must have been a busy man for that hour considering that the fish was fresh from the water. But our minds were much relieved to see how we had misjudged him.

Top right: Tête Jaune Cache [1908]

MARY SCHÄFFER FONDS (V527/PS I – IIO)*

47.

Later we were invited to a wonderful dinner of boiled beans, dried apple-sauce, bacon, fish and sour-dough – all in honor of the first white women these men had met in the Cache. They were prospectors from the eastern states and two exceptionally fine men. This was the fish and they had broiled it over wood. How we did enjoy that dinner and how we did talk of all the people and things we know of in the east. Alas, I believe the old Cache is no more. The railroad runs far on the hills above it, the people who go that way have no idea of the days when the Cache meant so much to the old fur trader. It was good to have seen it while even yet the shadow of the past lay upon it.

"Joe" and his big trout, n.d.

MARY SCHÄFFER FONDS (V527/PS I – 153)

185
🔱

Not till three years later did we see the mountains west of Edmonton again, and then it was to make a survey of Lake Maligne at the instigation of Dr. D.B. Dowling, one of the prominent Govt. surveyors. Things were frightfully changed. The Grand Trunk Pacific made us perfectly comfortable till we reached a point called Hinton. At this place our ponies were waiting for us and we started westward over a road well beaten down by teamsters hauling provisions and supplies for a trans-continental road. All Hinton was going west. It is a sight of which most of us have only read and I would not have missed this little bit of the passing of the West for a great deal.

Beef was going in on the hoof, thousands and thousands of animals. Magnificent horses were pulling patiently at the great loads of supplies. Women and children, babies and kitchen stoves filled still other huge vehicles. All were passing over a trail which had once known only the Indian moccasin, the men of the North-West Trading Co. and of the Hudson's Bay Co. We camped within sight of Roche Miette named in the early days and walked to the little cemetery near the old trading post known as Jasper House. In that open clearing, those silent graves, one could picture much of the old days. The long winter months, the great dog teams of furs, and the Indians coming to barter. What a picture it must have been. A little further west is the location of Henry House, the rival Co. of the Hudson's Bay. It is marked by the same open space and two fallen chimneys. Both locations are very close to the present village of Jasper, which came into existence with the coming of the railroads.

Graves at Jasper House

MARY SCHÄFFER FONDS (V527/PS 3 – 48)

49.

Here within sight of Roche Miette flows silently the great Athabaska. Beneath the shadow of that rock winds an old trail. Hunters have traversed it, the Indians and their dogs, the men of both companies – both gone. The march of progress has wiped out the poetry of living in these vast hills. It has also wiped out much hardship.

Right: [Roche Miette and Athabasca River]

MARY SCHÄFFER FONDS (DAMAGED) (V527/PS 3 – 49)

Opposite: Crossing Shovel Pass, 1911

MARY SCHÄFFER FONDS (V527/PS 1 – 132)*

50.

Only one sunny afternoon could be taken to study the locations which are not ancient history. We were bound for Maligne Lake with compass, log, tripod and even the lumber wherewith to build a boat from which to do our work. Our guide was a more or less skilled boatman and though he had cut and planed his lumber that not an extra ounce should be carried so far, he found it was going to be almost impossible to carry it over 30 miles of untouched ground. We had much for which to thank the Alberta Govt. who thought enough of our undertaking to loan us about ten men who went ahead cutting out sufficient undergrowth to allow our patient horse Jonas to carry his awkward loads safely to the shores of the lake. What a journey it was! Downhill, uphill, across rivers, someone had to be ahead of Jonas to balance his load. Once we nearly lost him in a mountain torrent, for no one could help him. He stood at the far bank, the boards caught in the bank, they balanced and swung, the water swept down and Jonas was trying to make his final spring to dry land. They swung up and down, Jonas began to look shaky round the legs, but at the psychological moment they swung up from the shore and Jonas (wise old thing) took his leap. This picture shows a hill looking toward the head waters of the Athabaska. Up this hill was slowly plodding the faithful Jonas carrying his clumsy burden of boards, while the rest of us dallied behind taking a few photos.

Making a trail in spring [on Shovel Pass], 1911

MARY SCHÄFFER FONDS (V527/PS I – 130)*

Here the outfit is shown getting through the soft snows of the Shovel Pass. By looking carefully, Jonas and his 16 ft. boards may be seen in the rear. He was always given the best that could be got. A very presentable trail would be ready for him in that sticky snow when all the other horses had tramped it down. Shovel Pass is not an authentic name, I think it is Big Horn, but the natives cling to the first name. As we had slowly made our way up the very snowy, wet incline, we suddenly spied two dark objects which the less-informed members of the party were sure were two sheep. Imagine our disgust on arriving at the place to find a couple of shovels which must have been hewn out by a skilful axe man. They had been left by the Govt. workers in case we got into trouble in the snow. None of our party could ever quite give up the old name which was tacked on it at the time.

Above: Looking toward Shovel Pass, 1911

MOORE FAMILY FONDS (V439/PS – 66)*

Right: [Shovels on Shovel Pass, 1911]

MARY SCHÄFFER FONDS (UNMOUNTED) (V527/PS I – 129)*

52.

The Shovel Pass route to the lake is well worth taking. It is about thirty miles long, and from the heights over which you travel there is a fine view of the lake. At the lower end of the lake the tents were pitched, the boat quickly constructed and the novel experience of surveying a lake without knowing how, was eventually done. We spent several weeks at it, but our tools were new to us, we made mistakes, but we also explored many side valleys, had many excursions and much pleasure.

Jonas & the boat on Shovel Pass, 1911

MARY SCHÄFFER FONDS (V527/PS I – 131)*

53.

The "Chaba Imne" (the old Indian name for the lake) was properly christened with an empty vinegar bottle. She was not built for beauty or speed but for service. She was capable of carrying all the dunnage, tents, cook-stove and five people from one end of the lake to the other and back, being out in two violent storms when none of the passengers ever expected to touch dry land again. The lake was proven to be 18 miles long. From the time a boat enters the "Narrows" there is a wealth of beauty to be found. At the upper end of the lake we found a fall playing only during the daytime and called it "Sunshine Falls." Doubtless it had its rise in some glacier behind "The Thumb." In the coves of the "Narrows" the wild duck nest, and there the ducklings take their first lessons in swimming. At the time of that last visit goat were very numerous on the eastern mountains about the lake. We had powerful glasses, and it was intensely interesting to watch all the families going to bed among the rocks with the setting of the sun.

There was a sigh of relief when the last day's notes of survey were taken, there was a sigh of regret that the camping days on that beautiful lake were over. Faithful "Chaba Imne" brought us clumsily for the last time into our small harbor and to our teepee home at the lower end of the lake just as night was falling

At the lower end of Maligne Lake

54.

Maligne Lake lies in the fastnesses of her hills, much more easily reached than in those days of toil, but no less fair than when we first saw her. You will find her worth a visit, whether bathed in morning sunshine, the noon's brightest glare or the setting of the sun.

Last night on Maligne [Lake]

MARY SCHÄFFER FONDS
(V527/PS I – 180)*

The End
Mary S. Warren
Banff, Alta.

THE CALL OF SWEET VOICES, CANNIBALS AND HEADHUNTERS

Winter in Asia, 1908

The Ainu of Japan

Following Edward S. Morse's visits to Japan beginning in 1877, and the release of his book *Japan Day by Day*, there was a resurgence of interest in the mysterious east. Morse was one of the first directors of the Peabody Museum in Salem, Massachusetts. Coincidentally, he was also the grandfather of Catharine Robb Whyte, founder of the Whyte Museum of the Canadian Rockies. In 1877 Morse visited Japan in search of coastal brachiopods, a phylum of marine animals, of which most species went extinct over 250 million years ago. His visit turned into a three-year stay when he was offered a post at the University of Tokyo.

Morse went on to recommend several fellow Americans as *o-yatoi gaikokujin* (hired foreigners) to support the modernization of the Meiji Era. He opened the study of archaeology and anthropology in Japan by discovering the Omori shell mound and researching material culture. He collected over 5,000 pieces of Japanese pottery for

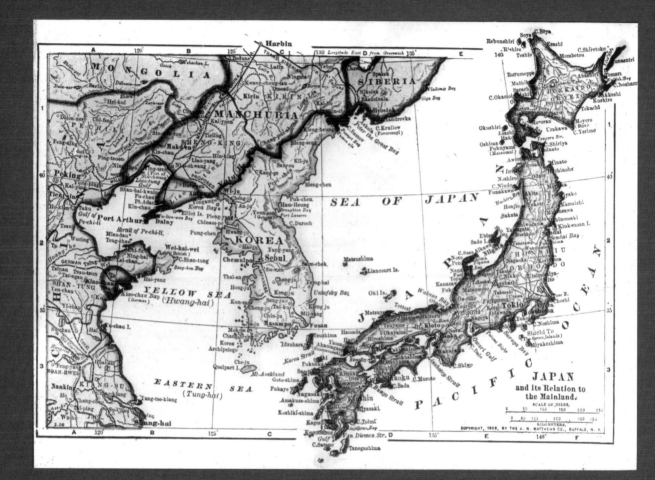

JAPAN
and its Relation to
the Mainland.

雨夜原柳

Opposite: Maps Japan and its relation to the Mainland

Above: Night Rain in Yanahala

museums in the eastern United States. While in Japan he authored a book on Japanese homes and their surroundings illustrated with his own line drawings. He also documented his observations of daily life in *Japan Day by Day*. His books raised a great deal of interest in Japan amongst Americans. Mary Schäffer was one of those Americans whose curiosity was piqued.

As mentioned earlier, during the winter of 1908 Mary Schäffer and Mollie Adams set out with two other friends, Miss Bippinorth and Miss McDonald, to visit Japan as guests of the Japanese government. Although she was happy to visit Tokyo, the temples at Nikko and other tourist destinations, Mary was determined to go beyond the typical Japanese tourist sites. She was particularly resolute to make contact with the indigenous people of Japan, the Ainu, and she strongly voiced her desire to her guides. Her insistence led her party to Hokkaido, where much to Mary's delight they were able to visit an Ainu village. Her

lantern slides are an amazing record of their journey to discover the Ainu of Japan.

The word "Ainu" means "human." The Ainu, also called the Ezo in historical texts, are the indigenous people of Japan and Russia. Full-blooded Ainu are lighter-skinned than their Japanese neighbours and have more body hair. Hence, Mary refers to the "hairy Ainus." Originally, the Ainu were distributed in the northern and central islands of Japan, from Sakhalin and the Kuriles in the far north and east down through Hokkaido and into northern Honshu.

Traditional Ainu culture differed greatly from Japanese culture. Men never shaved after a certain age and had full beards and moustaches. The women tattooed their mouths and sometimes their forearms, a practice Mary found shocking. The Ainu were animists, believing that everything in nature has a *kamui* (spirit or god) on the inside. The traditional Ainu lived by fishing, hunting and gathering wild plants. The Ainu women engaged in agriculture as a secondary activity to supplement these other food supplies.

From the mid-1400s, the Ainu were oppressed and exploited by the Japanese. In 1899 the Japanese government passed an act labelling the Ainu as former aborigines. This resulted in the land on which the Ainu people lived being taken by the Japanese government. Under the government policy of assimilation, the Ainu were prohibited from observing their daily customs. Although they were granted automatic Japanese citizenship, the Ainu were increasingly marginalized and discriminated against. This remains a problem today, although in 2008 a bipartisan, non-binding resolution was approved by the Japanese Diet calling upon the government to recognize the Ainu people as indigenous to Japan and urge an end to discrimination against them.

From 1807 to 1931, during which the Japanese started a census, the Ainu population decreased from 26,256 to 15,969. Although there are still some Ainu living on Sakhalin Island, the only Ainu speakers remaining now live solely in Japan and are concentrated primarily on the southern and eastern shores of Hokkaido. Although there is confusion as to the exact number of living indigenous people because those with indigenous backgrounds have hidden their identities due to ethnic issues, a 1984 census recorded Hokkaido's Ainu population at 24,381. Because of intermarriage, there are no truly Ainu settlements remaining.[95]

In her writings Mary remarked often on the strangeness of the people and places she passed, but she was as much a curiosity to the indigenous people in Japan and Taiwan as they were to her. Mary and her companions were sometimes forced to lower the blinds on their train windows against the prying eyes of the locals.

Sometime following her visit, Mary's article about their adventures, "With the Hairy Ainus," was published in the magazine *Travel and Exploration*.[96] The original article included only four images. It is reprinted in the following chapter, along with many more of Mary's lantern slide images from the Whyte Museum's collection.

With the Hairy Ainus, by Mrs. M.T.S. Schäffer

We judge the ignorance of others by our own lack of knowledge. Some years ago, influenced by the general revival of interest in things Japanese, I began to delve into the mine of history and literature relating to the island empire. Needless to say, much of interest relating to the arts, history, customs and surprising political development of this oriental people rewarded my efforts. One result of these casual investigations was the knowledge that a considerable remnant of that interesting Aboriginal race, the Ainus, was still to be found on the island of Yezo in the extreme north. Hence it came about that when I landed in Japan and was asked by a resident what most I wished to see: "Fuji, temples of course, and some of the lakes and mountains," I made answer: "Also, if it is possible, and if you please, I should much like to see the Ainus."

With so much of really great and accessible beauty to be viewed for the asking, this perhaps unreasonable request was met with such a look of pity and tolerance as boded ill for its realization. They showed us Nikko and her lovely hills, her lake and autumn foliage.

Below: Sacred Bridge, Nikko [1908]
MARY SCHÄFFER FONDS (v527/ps 1 – 1042)

Opposite: Sacred Bridge at Nikko [1908]
MARY SCHÄFFER FONDS (v527/ps 1 – 861)

Above: Kegon Falls – Nikko, Japan
[1908]

MARY SCHÄFFER FONDS (v527/ps I – 1024)

Left: A street in Nikko at night
[1908]

MARY SCHÄFFER FONDS (v527/ps I – 860)

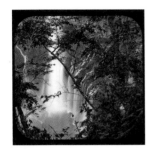

Above: Devil's Pit –
Nikko [1908]

MARY SCHÄFFER FONDS
(V527/PS I – 1025)

Right: Gamman ga
Fuchi Buddhas by the
Daiya River –
Nikko [1908]

MARY SCHÄFFER FONDS
(V527/PS I – 862)

206

Chuzenji near Nikko [1908]

*Cryptomarias on Old Tokkaido [Tokaido] Road
[1908]*

*We beheld the ancient temples and wonder-
ful cryptomeria tress, both there and on the old
Tokaido Road; yet still we held out for a peep into
the Ainu country.*

Mayanoshita, Hakone, cryptomarias [1908]

And at last, though the season (the middle of November) was exceedingly late for the expedition, a delightful companion and interpreter was found for us, Miss Kawai, a graduate of Bryn Mawr College, and we set forth to plunge immediately into the by-ways of Japanese travel, and to beard the Ainu in his native haunts. I fortified myself with a few historical facts about these people, gleaned from the Rev. John Batchelor's well-known "The Ainu and His Folk-lore." Mr. Batchelor has spent more than thirty years among the Ainus as a missionary, and has had, of course, exceptional opportunities for studying their lives and customs.

We learn from ancient Japanese chroniclers, as far back as 712 A.D., that these gentle, harmless people were at one time a race of savage cannibals. To-day they number about sixteen thousand souls, timid and harmless, and dying off fast. A few more years and the Ainu will be but a memory – so disappears the Aborigine. At one time inhabiting the entire island of Japan (as is proved by

ancient implements and names of places left behind), they have been gradually driven further and further north by the energetic invaders, till crossing Tsugaru Straits, they have taken their last refuge in the inhospitable hills of the Hokkaido. Their rapid decrease is said to be due originally to strife among the various clans; also from having been forced into vegetarianism when they are a race of hunters, as the Government has stopped the killing of deer, and their fishing-stations have been taken from them.

The most marked physical characteristic of the Ainu is the enormous growth of hair on the men, while the women are hideously tattooed on face and arms. The origin of this custom is lost in antiquity, though at the present day it is supposed to ward off disease. The skin surrounding the mouth of a young girl is early subjected to the ordeal by a tattoo made from the soot and juice of the birch bark, while on the day of her betrothal, the disfigurement is complete. A double moustache is the

result, if such a thing
can be imagined, being
a line of black below the
lower lip curving up-
ward, and joining the
line of a true mous-
tache about one inch
beyond the corner of
the mouth, while the
hands and arms receive
even more attention in
elaborately worked-out
patterns.

Ainus [1906]

4009 A SPLENDID TYPE OF
THE AINU ABORIGINE, AND HIS
FAMILY, ISLAND OF YEZO, JAPAN,
H.C. WHITE CO.
MARY SCHÄFFER FONDS
(V527/PS I – 841)

Opposite: Ainus [1906]

4007 AINU MEN THE
ABORIGINES OF JAPAN, IN FEAST
ATTIRE, ISLAND OF YEZO,
H.C. WHITE CO.
MARY SCHÄFFER FONDS
(V527/PS I – 838)

Above: [Ainu women in ceremonial dress, 1908]   *Opposite: Ainus [1908]*

The lip-tattoo differs from the tattoo of the savage women of Formosa, in that with the Ainu it ends in a graceful point at the lips, while with the Formosans it continues as a straight bar from the corners of the mouth to the ears.

The first sight of these Ainu women gave me the impression of having come across a lot of men masquerading as women, so masculine is the appearance of this tattoo on the lips.

One learns that they are an intensely superstitious race by glancing through Mr. Batchelor's book (but, then, what savage race is not?) and much of his good work has doubtless been lost owing to the mass of superstition with which he must be constantly coming in contact.

An enthusiastic worker among them told me of their intense fatalism, citing the instance of an old couple to whom she had daily made her way in the dead of winter, trudging through snow on her knees. The old man was ill, the woman indisposed. A doctor was brought with difficulty, the old man

Old Ainu [1908]

MARY SCHÄFFER FONDS (V527/PS I 844)

recovered; the old woman decided her time had arrived, refused to eat, to rouse herself, to do anything but die, and die she did in about two weeks with nothing the matter with her.

The poor Ainu is also troubled with a weakness common to many of his more civilized

Hot-springs Hotel on Hokkaido [1908]

brethren – he has an inordinate love of strong drink, and this failing probably as much as anything else, is assisting in his rapid extermination.

For a long time after the Ainu had settled on the island of Yezo, he was left much to himself, but Yezo is far too rich in natural resources to be longer neglected as a wilderness, and the Japanese are constantly pouring in and pushing him rapidly back into the, as yet, almost inaccessible hills.

As I said before, it was the middle of November before our party of three was ready to start for Hokkaido. Lying as it does between the 40th and 50th parallels, a tiny island, swept by icy winds of the north, we felt well assured of a more or less cold reception, so went thoroughly equipped with furs and blankets.

The ordinary tourist in Japan sees little of real Japanese conditions of travel, as in the central and southern parts of the island, where the "foreigner" wanders most, European hotels and customs have been largely introduced.

The rail-roads throughout the entire empire are narrow-gauge. I usually find that if traveling facilities are not as we are accustomed to in our own country, we are uncomfortable, so we were uncomfortable. But barring generally cramped conditions of the cars, eating cold lunches on the train, with insufficient heat in the daytime, and a thorough baking in the sleepers at night, our greatest trial was the frank curiosity of the populace who, accustomed only to an occasional passing missionary, peered into the low windows of the train till we were forced to draw down the blinds, or followed us in generous squads, making plenty of personal remarks which we fortunately could not understand.

The boat from Aomori to Hakodate was a surprisingly fine one, considering how far we were from the beaten way, and we will all long remember that six hours' sail across the quiet straits, when we followed the silver path of the moon, then glided into the dark harbor of Hakodate where only a few sleepy lanterns bobbed about, proclaiming it was a harbor at all.

Neither the primitive Japanese inn with its rather scanty mats spread on the floor for sleeping, nor the one general trough in the public hall where all were expected to wash, nor even the boiled

Railway car 84 for Hamamatsu Railway car 70 [1908]

MARY SCHÄFFER FONDS
(v527/ps 1 – 877)

At the Train [1908]

H.C. WHITE CO.
MARY SCHÄFFER FONDS
(v527/ps 1 – 878)

216

rice and raw fish for breakfast, failed to dampen our ardor to penetrate further to the haunts of the Ainu.

A morning's journey by train brought us to Sapporo, where is established a well-equipped university, which we visited, and also called upon Mr. Batchelor, previously mentioned. Unfortunately he was not at home, but his wife kindly gave us all the information she could, telling us that "Piratori was the best place to see these strange people, but of course it was out of the question, owing to the difficulties of getting there."

Miss Kawai, however, failed to recognize such things as "difficulties," and having laid our plan of action, we laid in a stock of necessary provisions, and started off the next day for our goal – Piratori, one of the most typical Ainu villages left.

About noon we emerged from the little rickety train, half passenger, half freight, at a station whose name translated is "Edge-of-the-Marsh." Here two sturdy peasant girls gathered up our rugs and valises, and proudly preceded us down the one street to the solitary village inn. Men, women and children paused as though struck dumb at such a sight, for except an occasional missionary, foreigners are undoubtedly scarce in that portion of the globe. The inn was tiny, rather clean and the ever-prevalent teapot of green tea was at our elbow before our hat-pins were removed.

Japanese bed [1908]

218

[Mary's basha ride, 1908]

MARY SCHÄFFER FONDS (V527/PS I – 951)

To the next station or village was a matter of
sixteen miles, and the only way to reach it was
by basha. To explain a basha to the uninitiated, I
should say it was a kind of cart of very limited
proportions, made of very good material about two
hundred years ago, put into use at that time, used
ever since and still fulfilling its vocation. One of

Main St. of Piritori and our basha – or coach [1908]

MARY SCHÄFFER FONDS (V527/PS I – 1007)

these antiquities stood at the door of the inn, but
as we were the only three, and the basha held six,
and there was a "horse-fair on at Piratori," the driver wished us to wait till he had gathered up three
more occupants. However, as the weather was cold,
the way long, the day half gone, and we none too
anxious for other company, he volunteered to start

[Meeting on the road, 1908]

MARY SCHÄFFER FONDS (V527/PS I – IOII)

providing we paid the extra fares – a matter of $1.50. This we gladly did, and piled in, as queer, shaggy, ratty, all-head and no-tail horses were attached to our crazy-looking equipage. With a whoop and the flourish of a green poplar stick with a string on the end of it as a lash, we scattered the children and chickens before us like chaff before wind, the innkeeper and his servants were left smiling and bowing far behind, and we went flying off into space as it were, in a deafening clatter of old harness, loose wheels, and flapping cotton curtains of the basha. That first basha ride is pounded indelibly into the memory as well as the flesh; nor can we banish the recollection of our driver, whom we soon dubbed "Cyclops," for he never failed to take the deep ruts of that marsh road with a rickety bound, then turned his one awful, red eye round to see how we took his horsemanship. At seven that night, after dragging through miles of deep sea-sand (we were following the coastline for two hours), he flourished the string whip one last time, lashed and switched the old broken reins, again sent the inhabitants, children, chickens and pigs in all directions, and came bounding and careering into village No. 2, drawing up at the aristocratic hostelry of that hamlet.

Tired and cramped we tumbled out, wondering where the driver could have stowed the three other passengers we had paid for. Having with narrow escapes preserved our necks on this day's ride, we engaged him for the morrow, and as the horses

had only tried to run away once, we engaged them too! The Japanese supper of delicious fresh fish (caught only a mile away), and served with rice and chopsticks, tasted good indeed after our strenuous exercise, while a little later the wadded mats both under and over us, drove bashas from the brain for the next eight hours.

By dawn the next morning we were up, buttoning buttons with aching fingers and eating fish soup and cold lobster over a handful of charcoal. Cyclops appeared at seven with

221

[Horses with basha in Piratori, Japan, 1908]

his team and aged basha and off we went on the last lap for the Ainu village.

This time we carried an extra passenger, a sweet young girl who, almost totally blind, was making her way home from the hospital as well as she could, and with whom she could.

Though I could understand no word she spoke, her voice was low and sweet and musical, and the pathetic story of her life was afterwards repeated to me. Dressed in the garb of the Japanese, with a certain amount of education, minus the usual tattooing, she showed the good result of missionary work among these people.

We began passing Ainu afoot and on horse-back; they were easily distinguished from the Japanese by the masses of hair and beard of the men, and the tattooed mouths of the women. Their form of stirrup was rather curious. To the very primitive bridle they attached a string or light rope, which fell each side of the horse's neck with a loop in each end. Into these loops the bare feet were thrust just far enough for the toes to clutch the rope, and there they held on, as sure of their perch as though safely ensconced in a Mexican saddle. We were also surprised to see what remarkably fine horses they were riding. These animals are very superior in appearance to those on the main Island of Japan, a circumstance probably due to the fact that Japan is a country without grass, while the verdure of Hokkaido resembles more our own temperate zone.

Our road was taking us deeper into the hills. The scenery grew more wild as we advanced, scrub oak covered the scantily cleared portions of the country, and forests of magnificent oak trees, festooned with mistletoe, spread before us and disappeared into indefinite distances. The wind whistled and shrieked around the old basha, our fingers and toes needed no thermometer to prove to us that it was decidedly below freezing point, and yet on the bleak coast and sweep of wooded mountain we saw not a chimney, not a curl of smoke to proclaim an open wood fire or a stove. The Ainu seem to have adopted the Japanese form of heating – the hibachi and its handful of charcoal.

We came to the little paddock where the horse-fair was being held, and one glimpse proved that horse-fairs are the same in savage as well as civilized countries. The men were strolling among the stock, or leaning nonchalantly over the fence chewing a straw and assuming the same air of indifference which they do at home, when they have their eye on the best horse in the bunch, and mean to get it for nothing! Filled with his own sense of importance and horsemanship, Cyclops allowed us but a peep of this pastoral scene, and having jogged along for an hour almost asleep, he suddenly roused himself, and violently beating the

Top right: Ainu Women – Piritori – 1908

MARY SCHÄFFER FONDS (V527/PS I – 837)

Right: [Ainu man and horse in Piritori, 1908]

MARY SCHÄFFER FONDS (V527/PS I – 868)

astonished horses, went careering down into the village of Piratori. Here we hauled up in front of the only dirty Japanese inn we encountered on the entire trip (the poorest of them are so invariably immaculate) and crawled out stiff and cold to see as much as we could in the short time at our disposal. The village was about half a mile long; and houses thatched similarly to those of the Japanese peasantry further south, lined both sides of the solitary street.

Where a home stood, the granary or storehouse would usually be on the opposite side of the road,

Top right: [Ainu peasant, 1908]

MARY SCHÄFFER FONDS (V527/PS I – 869)

Right: [Woman in front of haystack, 1908]

MARY SCHÄFFER FONDS (V527/PS I – 1009)

Opposite: Ainu store-houses [1908]

MARY SCHÄFFER FONDS (V527/PS I – 845)

and to prevent the ravages of rat, was built four to six feet from the ground.

The Formosan savages have practically the same structures, except for the addition of a circular wooden disc at the top of each support, as further protection against rodents.

Women and little children rapidly gathered about us, not with the crowding and pushing of the low-class Japanese, but gently and good-naturedly. Again I was impressed with the sweetness of their voices, and no stretch of the imagination could make me think of them as descendants of cannibals. Water was evidently not their strong point, it seldom is in the lower planes of life, but in natural politeness they certainly excelled.

Very willingly they allowed us to use the camera, and proved immensely proud of their tattooing, especially the hands, which they placed conspicuously in front when asked to pose. Their needle work is exceedingly crude, a form of appliqué of blue cotton cloth on white being all that I saw. They also

[Children in Piratori, 1908]

weave a very poor material from elm bark with which they make their summer garments. Young children are carried on the back swung from a guard which passes across the forehead, their grain is ground by hand in huge stone mortars, chickens were in evidence, and altogether they were the most civilized savages I had ever seen. This had no doubt been brought about by their contact with the

226

Ainu children crushing grain [1908]

Japanese, with whom they are now intermarrying and whose children they frequently adopt.

Probably one of the most marked peculiarities of the Ainu is their worship of the bear as a totem. These animals are so numerous in the Hokkaido, that the Japanese, who have established themselves there for the purpose of stock-raising, lose many valuable animals in the course of the early spring.

The Ainu's greatest delight is to capture a cub. The little chap is then brought up with the children of the village, till hugs and claws become dangerous, when he is caged, and kept till three or four years of age. Then takes place a curious religious ceremony, in which the bear is most cruelly killed, after which a feast is prepared, prayers offered to the victim, ending up with dancing and great rejoicing.

Having heard so much of this bear worship, we were astonished to find at the time of our visit to Piratori, the village could boast no bear. Later we found that a missionary had established herself in the town, and it may be through her influence that this part of their barbaric life has been abandoned, as Mr. Batchelor himself refers to this custom as one of the greatest barriers to his work among them.

As the afternoon advanced, the cloud thickened, the wind grew more bitterly cold, and even the small unheated inn fifteen miles away, was a cheerful thought in comparison to the old springless basha, the miles of hills and hollows ahead of us, and the icy blast we must face.

A few little children and the inevitable chickens saw us off, the horse-fair was still in progress, the wind shrieked through the vast oak forests and it was dusk as the weary little nags forded the river and landed us, chilled to the bone, at the door of the inn. We had seen the Ainu.

[Map of Taiwan]

MARY SCHÄFFER FONDS (V527/PS 1 – 908)

In 1908 Mary Schäffer and her travelling companions also visited Formosa, now known as Taiwan, when it was under Japanese rule. Formosa was always a popular place to conquer because of its important location along shipping routes. The Japanese officially took over Taiwan in 1895 and stayed for 50 years. They left after losing the Second World War. Upon their departure the Chinese Nationalist Party took over.

In Formosa Mary was again determined to visit indigenous peoples. The indigenous peoples in Taiwan belong culturally and linguistically to the Austronesian group. The distribution of the Austronesian group originates in Taiwan in the north, extends to Easter Island in the east and to Madagascar in the west. Some common characteristics of traditional Austronesian peoples are building houses on stilts to protect against the damp, insects and snakes; adopting slash-and-burn farming techniques; chewing betel nuts; weaving bamboo and rattan; and relying on hunting and fishing. In Taiwan, 13 indigenous tribes are still known today. It is likely that there were more tribes in Mary's time, as occupation encroached upon the lands and livelihood of indigenous people and some tribes disappeared as a result, although the time of their disappearance is not clear. Mary's interest in indigenous peoples led her to visit two of the tribes that still exist today, the Atayal and the Amis.

Traditionally, the Atayal believe they were born from stones. They have a customary set of shared taboos and beliefs called *gaga* that is unique to them. If *gaga* is violated, they believe they will be punished by the spirits. They also share a belief in *Rutux*, a supernatural spiritual being. The Atayal practise facial tattooing both as a form of beauty and as protection from evil spirits. The tattooing represents a mastery of embroidery for women and courage in men. It is also a totem for recognizing the ancestors. The Atayal are also the only tribe that tattoo, mostly on the face. Some Atayal live traditionally today, but as with indigenous people the world over, many traditions are lost through assimilation.

At the time of Mary's visit, there were several tribes that practised headhunting, including the Atayal, Bunong and Paiwan tribes. Mary refers to the Atayal as one of the most ferocious tribes. Earlier in the book, I mentioned my chance meeting with Beki Hunt in France, the woman whose partner, Amour Lee, is from the Amis people. They told me that although much of the information about the Atayal tribe indicates they were the fiercest, the aborigines would not consider

themselves fierce. One of the reasons for headhunting was to make offerings to the gods. It also demonstrated bravery and showed the ability of the hunters to protect their tribe. As the Amis were encouraged or forced to assimilate throughout the first half of the twentieth century, headhunting was no longer considered an acceptable practice by the dominant cultures.

231

Central Ataials [Atayals] [1908]

MARY SCHÄFFER FONDS (V527/PS 1 – 889)

232

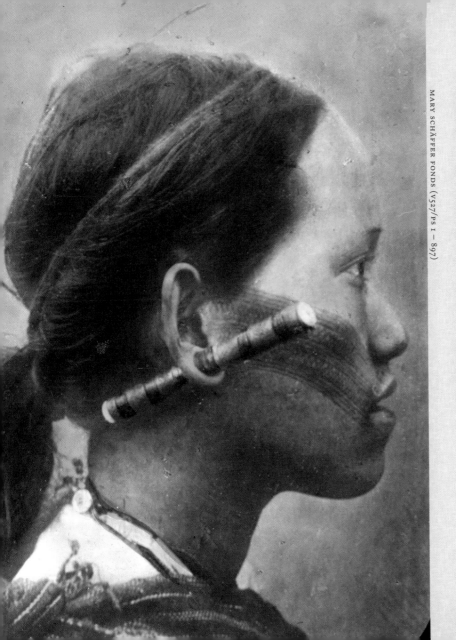

Opposite: South Ataials [Atayals] –
Formosa [1908]

Left: North Ataials [Atayals] [1908]

Above: Central Ataials [Atayals],
Formosa [1908]

The traditional Amis society is matrilineal and the matriarch decides household affairs. Traditionally, men are involved in tribal politics, fishing and architecture. The Amis tribe has an age-graded organization. When boys reach the age of 13 or 14, they are required to enter a youth organization to receive adulthood training, including strict physical and martial training. They are known for their music and vibrant clothing. These would have been common practices during Mary's time and some Amis still live traditionally today.

234

East Coast Ami [Amis] – Formosa [1908]

There are some interesting references to individual indigenous people in Mary's article. For example, she describes a man selling bananas. It is an odd description in that Mary refers to the man's eyes as beady and constantly shifting. I wondered if she had misinterpreted his body language. For example, it is impolite for many First Nations people in Canada to make eye contact, so white people sometimes translated this by our standards as being shifty behaviour. I asked my Amis friend Amour Lee if Mary may have misunderstood the man's body language. He told me that in the past the Aboriginals considered it rude to look you straight in the eye. Mary also comments on the small size of the bananas, but my friend said, "The part about the bananas is funny to me because bananas here are much smaller compared to the North American standard, but they are actually much tastier!"

Some of the tribes that still existed during Mary's time no longer exist today, including the

School children of the Tappo Savage group in Mount Ari, Formosa [1908]

MARY SCHÄFFER FONDS (V527/PS I – 1037)

Pingpu tribe from Northern Taiwan. As in Japan, there is confusion in Taiwan as to the exact number of indigenous people living on the island, because, like the Ainu, they were encouraged to deny their ethnic origins in the dominant culture's push to assimilate them.

235

The story of the Amis people is tragically similar to that of other Aboriginal people the world over. Amour Lee's grandmother still speaks her native language and lives traditionally. His parents were afraid to admit their heritage. Amour learned to speak Taiwanese and Mandarin and he was instructed by his parents not to admit his roots for fear of discrimination. Forced assimilation has led to the loss of a diversity of cultures throughout the world.

On the same 1908 trip to Asia, Mary wrote an article entitled "A Glimpse of the Head-hunters of Formosa." She may have written it with the intention of publication, but this article was never published. It does, however, provide insight into Mary's adventures that are amusing and enlightening. This article gives a much deeper and more personal sense of the author's experiences than the published "With the Hairy Ainus."

A Glimpse of the Head-hunters of Formosa
by Mary T.S. Schäffer

The history of Formosa before 1895 is little more than one of blood-shed and strife. In that year when he passed it over to Japan, Li Hung Chang remarked – "You take the island, but with it a curse from which you will never free yourselves – brigandage."[97]

On assuming power, the Japanese promptly met every case of such outrage with decapitation, with the result that today there is not a brigand left on the island. Japan was making her first bow to the world as a colonist, and comparing the present results with the history before 1895, she may feel justly proud of her experiment. As far back as 611 A.D., Chinese history records the savages of that island as exceptionally cruel. Chinese and Japanese were constantly contesting for possession, and pirates of

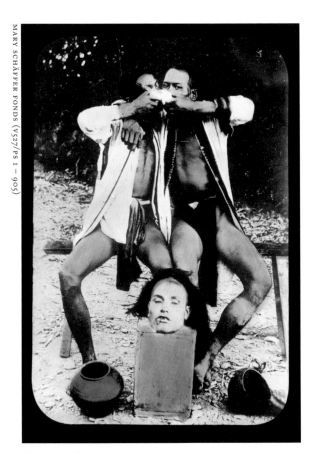

Formosa [1908]

both nations robbed and murdered, while crimi-
nals from both lands found it a safe abiding place
from the law.

For years the Portuguese, Dutch, Spanish, Japanese
and Chinese fought for the island, till about the beginning of the 17th century, when the Chinese became the acknowledged government. From then
on, the island with its native savages and the very
scum of both Chinese and Japanese races became a
menace to every vessel plying the dangerous waters
surrounding that coast.

Repeatedly Japan and other nations urged pun-
ishment for the atrocious murders of ship-wrecked
sailors, but China remained inert. By 1875 she
roused from her lethargy and realized that unless
serious steps were taken, some one of the powers
would wrest the little island from her. It was then
that Taihoku was made the capital, a governor installed for some months of the year, and a high
wall erected around the city for protection against
savages and the hordes of brigands. Today the high

237

walls have disappeared, gone with the brigands, while the savages are being slowly and firmly driven further and further into the fastnesses of the mountain range which extends the length of the island. The cultivation of tea and rice on the open plains of the west coast, both in the northern and central sections of the island, is rapidly extending, and the sugar industry in the south is rapidly driving out all other products. The oranges and bananas, while not made a feature of the country, we found most delicious. The almost inaccessible hills are covered with superb timber, the camphor trees alone bringing an enormous revenue even with the present precarious conditions surrounding the workers.

The method for handling savages is more or less unique. An imaginary

Above: Rice Fields in Formosa [Taiwan] Hills [1908]

MARY SCHÄFFER FONDS (V527/PS I – 883)

Opposite: [Ploughing rice fields – Formosa, 1908]

MARY SCHÄFFER FONDS (V527/PS I – 885)

and in places, a very realistic line is drawn, beyond which they must not venture. Police stations are disposed along the line at intervals, throughout the entire route from north to south, in which telephone and telegraph systems have been installed, thus giving to the brave, isolated men stationed in them to enforce obedience, communication with each other and the outside world; and there they remain (some with their families) liable at any moment, night or day, to the attacks of the savages.

Those savages who will come in and surrender to the law, are treated with kindness and consideration; and it is some of these we hoped to see on our short visit to Formosa.

Our entrance into Kelung harbor, though in a downpour of rain, recalled the significance of the name given to the Island by the Portuguese – Formosa – "Beautiful Island." The low surrounding hills were covered from base to summit with a tropical growth of waving palms, tree-ferns and

Wire Entanglements against the Savages in the BonBon Valley, Formosa [1908]

bamboo. Chinese sampans with great eyes painted on the bows (the Chinese say a boat needs eyes to move), manned by little yellow fellows in queues[98] and grass capes, skimmed over the waters like mosquito-catchers on a still pond. Everyone was busy with the arrival of our steamer.

Above: Takow [Kaohsiung] [1908]

MARY SCHÄFFER FONDS (V527/PS I – 902)

Left: Takow [Kaohsiung] [1908]

MARY SCHÄFFER FONDS (V527/PS I – 914)

A few minutes' walk from the wharf to the train which was to take us to Taihoku, the capital, brought us to the little first-class car, dripping from head to heels, consoled with the information that "Kelung boasts the fourth-largest rainfall in the world." So little is as yet written of Formosa, that our first glimpse of the island, as we rushed along through the country in those narrow-gauge cars, was probably one of the most interesting experiences of our two weeks' stay. The first sight of

Above: [Water Buffalo in Formosa, 1908]

MARY SCHÄFFER FONDS (V527/PS I – 923)

the famous tea-growing country, the queer clusters of Chinese houses and their peaked roofs, the rank tropical growth, the garlands of purple flowers festooning the rail-road banks – ferns, ferns everywhere – the

Opposite: Old Gateway in Taihoku Wall [1908]

MARY SCHÄFFER FONDS (V527/PS I – 916)

mouse-colored water-buffalo plunging and wallowing through the long rows of mud and water, which would someday be respectable rice fields, the curious old graveyards here and there – it was all a strange panorama indeed.

Top left: Chinese Houses – Taihoku [1908]

Above: Old Gateway in Taihoku Wall [1908]

Left: [Taihoku, Formosa – Old Gateway Wall in background, 1908]

Opposite: In Taihoku [1908]

Above: New Year decorations at private residence in Taihoku, Formosa [1908]

MARY SCHÄFFER FONDS (V527/PS I – 924)

Right: Old Gateway of wall formerly around Taihoku [1908]

MARY SCHÄFFER FONDS (V527/PS I – 919)

An hour's run and then we arrived at Taihoku station to be met by and introduced to the gentleman who was to have us under his personal care for the next two weeks. For traveling in Formosa is no easy matter to the "foreigner" who has neither the Japanese nor the Chinese language at his command; and Count Sakuma, Governor General of the Island, had honored Dr. Nitobe by placing his personal interpreter at the disposal of Dr. Nitobe's friends.

Mr. Miyoshi, a graduate of Harvard College, a magnificent type of manhood both mentally and physically, assumed the rather trying position of escort to four "foreign" women with an absolutely unperturbed brow, a brow which shone with genial friendliness as the days went by. Taihoku proved a most interesting city, with her wide, well-paved streets, the now useless walls having been torn down and used as a basis for the good roads; while the governor's palace, fine public buildings and numerous public schools, proved a splendid example of Japan as a colonizer, and was a marvelous contrast to the mother country, who has much to eradicate before she can compare in sanitary conditions to her young child. The Chinese element predominated everywhere. Pretty Japanese ladies rode by in kurumas,[99] Chinese women were either being carried about in clumsy Chinese chairs, or toddled along on their terribly deformed feet, and the little children of both nations enjoyed our daily walks as much as we did ourselves.

St. [Street] in Taiwan [1908]

Not the least of our surprises was finding that the Taihoku Railroad Hotel was built and run on elaborate foreign lines, when we had set out to visit a "savage" country.

We were permitted, through courtesy of the Government, to visit the camphor and opium factories, which are both under its control. The camphor tree, which grows to enormous proportions on this island, and whose habitat is the mountainsides, is hewn down, chopped into tiny pieces, distilled, then carried down as crude oil in huge square cans on the backs of coolies to the factories in Taihoku, where it is refined and packed for

Top right: Shishunen – Four Springs Garden – Hotel at Tainan [1908]

MARY SCHÄFFER FONDS (V527/PS I – 858)

Right: Shishunen – Four Springs Garden – Hotel at Tainan [1908]

MARY SCHÄFFER FONDS (V527/PS I – 832)

the foreign markets. As the Japanese slowly advance their guards into the fastnesses of the savages, the camphor-workers keep pace with them, and many a poor wood-chopper loses his life as the savages sweep down upon the camps; and many a poor coolie swinging down the mountain trail with his two cans of fragrant oil lays down his burden and gives up his head to the covetous head-hunter. For be it known that no lover has proven his bravery and manhood till he can lay at the feet of his bride a Chinese head by preference – a Japanese head if the other is not forthcoming.

When we confided to our kind conductor that we aspired to a glimpse of the savage hills, as well as a burning desire to behold some of the more harmless of the savages themselves, he seemed utterly puzzled why four civilized women should voluntarily rush into a variety of hardships such as he hastened to enumerate in glowing colors. We met every obstacle with the query, "Can it be done with the retention of our heads?" He admitted it could, "At least a glimpse of one band might be had, who had surrendered some time previously." This band was a portion of the Atayals, the most northerly tribe on the island, and one of the most ferocious.

On the morning of Dec. 24, '08, with faces turned toward the mysterious mountain-range where these people dwell, we climbed

Traveling to Mitsui Camphor road. First part of journey to hills where savages dwell. Formosa [1908]

MARY SCHÄFFER FONDS (V527/PS I – IOI2)

into the tiny flat-cars belonging to the Mitsui Camphor Company, and set forth for the weirdest "unknown" we had yet experienced. Each car contained two passengers and was pushed by an energetic coolie ten miles over the wide, open valley.

251

Here we saw practically nothing of the peasant life of Japan, the people being mostly Chinese, with all the customs and conditions of that race. The cars being manned by excitable coolies and not the gentle Japanese, we went hurrying by tea fields, rice fields, sweet-potato fields. Kurumas and Chinese chairs were passed in the wink of an eye, small-footed mothers rushed to the doors of their squalid homes dragging unfortunate youngsters to behold the sight of four "foreign" women bounding and careering along in reckless fashion at the will of the excitable coolies, and even the phlegmatic water-buffalo halted his weary step and gazed stupidly after us. At one moment it seemed we must pitch into the ditch on our right, the next instant be sprawled on the rough stones of the roadside; but finding we were all there after each fright, we left our necks to the coolies and turned our attention to the scenery. The mountains seemed to creep nearer and nearer, the little two-foot track came to an abrupt end, and two forlorn Chinese chairs stood with cadaverous expressions awaiting

252

[Railway car to Mitsui Camphor road, 1908]

their reluctant load. The reputation of those chairs for cleanliness, and the Chinese who use them most, is rather unsavory, and only those who must, ever take them. One of our party bravely got in, our uncritical belongings were stowed in the other, and we set off on a ten-mile walk straight into the hills, the Tamsui River marking our general course.

[Chinese chair, 1908]

These hills seemed to be largely composed of excessively slippery clay; and though it had not rained for twenty-four hours, it was quite difficult to retain our footing at the steeper places; otherwise the trail was a perfectly good one, as well as novel to those accustomed to conditions in more northern zones.

The varieties of ferns seemed innumerable; strange plants constantly called a halt, bright butterflies flitted temptingly out of reach, the bamboos waved and nodded above us, and sweet voices of unknown birds greeted the strangers to this fairy-land.

Reaching the Mitsui Camphor Station, beyond which no-one passes without a permit, we drank tea, ate some delicious bananas grown on the spot and some hard-boiled duck eggs, and again started forward, this time accompanied by a guard. It began to look interesting, especially when a rock was pointed out to us with the information that only three years ago, seventy Chinese men, women and children had been murdered there by savages. We began to look for dark faces peering amidst the tall waving pampas grass, to see imaginary forms emerging from behind the rocks along the trail, and were requested "not to fall behind picking flowers, but to keep close together."

A swinging wire bridge, quite one hundred yards above the boiling Tamsui and fully two hundred yards long, "where a German army officer had shuddered and turned back," was the next point

of interest. One wondered at the officer's lack of nerve, for except having an inclination to sway and wobble considerably, it was safe enough for a blind man. As I looked back and saw our chair rider sailing serenely along, it seemed to me to need more nerve in that form than any other. Had the coolies been so minded, a twist of the wrist or a stumble would have sent her and the chair quite sheer of the guard wires into the depths below.

The trail wound on and on, growing higher, narrower and more wild and beautiful, till – we walked out upon an open spot where nestled a savage village.

The huts, thatched on the sides as well as the roofs, reminded us strongly of the Ainu huts in the Hokkaido; the features and complexes of the people bore an equally strong resemblance to the Ainu, but their costumes were entirely different, and there

Top left: Wire bridge over Tamsui River [Danshui] [1908]

MARY SCHÄFFER FONDS (V527/PS I – 926)

Left: Bridge over Tamsui River [Danshui]. Men carrying shoulder carriage over bridge [1908]

MARY SCHÄFFER FONDS (V527/PS I – 927)

Savage Village in Formosa [1908]

Formosan Savages in their Village [1908]

255

was not the mass of hair which is such a marked characteristic of the northern tribe. Trees and the heavy undergrowth had been burned away and here and there were small patches of cultivated ground – just about enough to prevent starving.

There was no doubt of the curiosity existent on both sides, but we were forced to hurry on, as the sun was slipping rapidly behind the towering hills. In another hour, passing a second collection of huts, crossing a wire bridge swinging high above a dark

China, Japan, Formosa, U.S., and Canada [1908]

ravine, we walked into the little police-station of Urai, the furthest point on this trail to which the cautious government has permitted a "foreigner" to penetrate. In that wild spot stood a tiny house clinging to the mountain-side for a mere existence, below plunged and pounded the Tamsui, behind us lay the villages of surrendered savages, and around us gathered the men whose duties kept them in this lonely region where danger faced them always.

Japan has paid a heavy toll for that which she had wrested from the hill tribes, and she will pay more before the forests are completely hers for commercial purposes. Removing our shoes from weary feet, we entered the small house to find it as most Japanese houses are, neat as a pin and the floor covered with soft mats. We were shortly escorted across the river by the guard to a charming pool of naturally hot water, when a delicious bath soon made us forget we had just finished a jaunt of ten miles over a steep mountain trail.

Then Christmas Eve closed down upon us, night wrapped us all, savage and civilized alike, in her cloak of darkness and our minds turned to supper. The outside screens were slipped into place, the shoji [in traditional Japanese architecture, a shoji is a

MARY SCHÄFFER FONDS (V527/PS I – 896)

Above: Hot Springs in Savage Hills Formosa [1908]

Opposite: Shishunen [note the shoji] [1908]

MARY SCHÄFFER FONDS (V527/PS I – 950)

door, window or room divider consisting of translucent paper over a frame and lattice of wood] closed about us, the eyes of the curious were upon us no longer. Cold meat, jam, stale bread, and tea formed that Christmas feast;

as we ate it sitting round the floor before a low table, it tasted good enough for the gods, so tired were we from the wild, wonderful, exciting tramp of the day. By eight, blankets were spread on the soft mats, "Saiunara" [Sayonara] was called from one tiny room to the other, and four weary people lay down in a row on the floor to dream of home across the water, and other Christmas Eves.

Suddenly a screen in the next room rattled, there was a low word from the guard, and the information came in through the paper wall – "He says not to mind the rats, that there were a good many about." We all sighed "Rats!" – and just hoped they would forget to come this night. Had we not been warned, [we] might easily have thought our neighbors across the gorge had come for our heads. To obtain more air in our tight quarters we had slipped the shoji to one side and then so many flocked in, they seemed to be all over the room, scaling the wall and floor, [they] raced and tore about, shrieked like mad things and behaved thoroughly

ratty – we all gave a nervous giggle. Growing accustomed to the racket, I was just dropping asleep when a rat stepped on my hair; raising a hand to drive him off, he leapt into some tea-cups at my head and china fell with a clatter.

Personally I burrowed further into my sleeping bag, forgot savages and rats alike, and only awoke at 6:30 A.M. to the old familiar call of "Merry Christmas!"

Breakfast was soon eaten of what the rats had left us; and though they had made sad havoc of our food and pressed plants, they fortunately spared our boots and clothing, and by 8 o'clock we were ready for the march.

Photographs of these strange people were my next desire, and it was most depressing to learn that the men of both villages had started at dawn on a deer-hunt. I think the news was a certain satisfaction to our escort, as he seemed to feel a little dubious of the reception which might be accorded our cameras.

The morning was perfect, we swung along at a brisk pace, meeting and passing the coolies with their aromatic loads of camphor-oil, and keeping one eye out for any strange native.

I was a little in advance of the others with the guard, when swinging round a sharp bend in the trail, I suddenly came upon a beautiful sight – a savage mother. On her back she carried a huge burden, and poised above it, a tiny child. She showed no fear of the camera, and accepted the small silver coin with a pretty smile.

A little lower down the hill, a man sat crouched on the high bank, with a native pipe in his mouth; huddled up in a little heap he sat there waiting for a prospective buyer of three green unhealthy-looking bananas. We

Formosa Savage on the trail [1908]

MARY SCHÄFFER FONDS (V527/PS I – 1045)

259

A Formosan Savage [1908]

bought the bananas, ditto the pipe, showed our silver, and got a picture. He was quiet but alert and watchful during the camera episode, the beady eyes constantly shifting from one to the other of us; and I felt a considerable satisfaction that the guard was at my elbow. His expression left slight doubts in my mind that the reverence for the law and order had not reached much beneath the skin.

We then arrived at the village we had first passed on our upward journey, took a number of pictures of the women, children and their huts,

[The banana man, 1908]

and obtained from them ear ornaments, necklaces, baskets and portions of dress. They were a genial, laughing crowd, apparently very glad to see us, and examined us as minutely as we did them. It did not take long to discover that they were quite enough in touch with the world to know silver from copper, and accepted only silver.

Obtaining all we could in photographs, we waved a gay goodbye, took up our march on the winding, flower-bedecked trail, and

Our boat on the Tamsui [Danshui] Rapids [1908]

descended to a boat-landing on the Tamsui where a Chinese sampan, manned by coolies, awaited us; we were thus to cut off five miles of tramping under the now broiling sun, by shooting the Tamsui rapids.

These rapids were ten in number, and I believe more or less dangerous; but crouched in the bottom of the boat away from the sweep of the long pole, we had no sense of fear. Our pilot stripped to the waist, and bending

gracefully to his oar, made a magnificent picture, as the body in its strength and self-confidence stood silhouetted in rich mahogany against the foam of the rapids.

Then in all too short a time the sampan glided up to the banks of the river above which clung the village of Shintan. We disembarked, found the queer little truck-cars awaiting us, then took a last, long look at the savage hills we were leaving, those hills peopled by a race so little known or understood, – a race which must live out the tragedy of defeat and extermination as Aboriginal tribes the world over have done before them.

263

Mary S. S. Schäffer

Above: Embarking for shooting the Tamsui [Danshui] Rapids, Formosa [1908]

Opposite: [On the river, 1908]

[Mary's visit to Asia ended tragically with the death of her dear friend and travelling companion Mollie Adams. Mollie died of pneumonia and Mary left her "sleeping in Kobi on the beautiful heights overlooking the Pacific."[100]]

A LIFE WELL LIVED

Hurtling along the Icefields Parkway by car today, I find it difficult to imagine that less than 100 years ago, there was no road connecting Banff, Alberta, to Mary's beloved Maligne Lake. Only by experiencing my own backcountry travel can I share her understanding of how access has changed these once-remote areas. But standing on the shores of Maligne Lake, it is easy to understand Mary's love for this beautiful place and her desire to preserve it as part of Jasper National Park. Her contribution to making this happen is a gift to all who visit today.

Mary's childhood sparked her interest in natural wonders, but it did not prepare her for the adventurous life and backcountry challenges she came to love. She chose to take full advantage of the freedom afforded her by travelling roads on which few had gone before. She came to believe that "nature meant us all to be wildflowers instead of house-plants."[101] Her marriage to Charles Schäffer fuelled her interest in botany and encouraged her to become a better artist and photographer. But it was her natural curiosity and love of learning that led her to explore the untracked wilderness of the Canadian Rockies, to develop friendships with indigenous people and to travel the world seeking new experiences.

Mary's interest in indigenous people took her off the beaten track in Canada, Japan and Formosa, now Taiwan. Her photographs of these people demonstrate her ability to put her subjects at ease. Although her imperialistic views and language offend contemporary sensibilities, her writing shows empathy for the plight of indigenous peoples around the world. Her writing also provides a glimmer of understanding of the impact that colonization has had on indigenous people.

Very little was done during Mary's time to rectify the impact of colonization on indigenous people around the world, but there has since been some progress toward developing a better understanding of these issues. Attempts have been made to improve conditions for indigenous people over the past 50 years. There are, for example, ongoing efforts in Canada to redress such wrongs of colonization as the residential school system. However, our current understanding of indigenous people gives us little right to impose our contemporary values on Mary's worldview. Our ongoing desire in North America for more of everything will continue to take an irreversible toll on the environment, destroying the diversity of both natural and human systems. Mary's views may pale in comparison to our values today when scrutinized by future generations.

Mary's interest in history led her to follow the footsteps of earlier adventurers and explorers. She gained first-hand knowledge of the places she had once discovered only through reading. The sad loss of her dear travelling companion Mollie Adams slowed Mary down for a while, but it also urged her to put pen to paper. Through her writing, she encouraged others to overcome their own fears and to risk venturing into unknown places.

The year 1911 was one of landmarks for Mary. *Old Indian Trails of the Canadian Rockies* was published; she returned with Caroline and Paul Sharpless to survey Maligne Lake, which ultimately led to its inclusion in Jasper National Park; and an opportunity arose to obtain land in Banff, enabling her to relocate. In Banff Mary would continue to share her love of wildlife and wild land in her writing and lantern slide presentations. Even when she could no longer undertake long backcountry travels, she lived a full life as an active member of the Banff community.

Mary died of pneumonia in her Banff home on January 23, 1939. Her roots here were not deep, but like a tree in the high alpine, they gained a widespread hold in the Banff community. There is much physical evidence of Mary's influence: Tarry-a-while, the home built for her by her "Chief," Billy Warren, now owned by the Peter and Catharine Whyte Foundation; a stained glass window in St. George's-in-the-Pines Anglican Church that she dedicated to her dear friend and guide Sid Unwin; her legacy of lantern slides, writings and artifacts in the Whyte Museum of the Canadian Rockies archives and finally, her gravestone in the Banff cemetery where she now rests amongst her kindly neighbours. She has found the peace she sought.

Stained glass window at St. George's-in-the-Pines Anglican Church in Banff that Mary dedicated to her friend Sid Unwin

Mary's grave in the Banff cemetery

1 Schäffer Warren to Raymond Zilmer, April 12, [1928?], Whyte Museum of the Canadian Rockies, M8/accn. 6081.

2 Ibid.

3 Schäffer Warren to Raymond Zilmer, January 2, n.d., Whyte Museum of the Canadian Rockies, M8/accn. 6081.

4 It is generally believed that Maligne Lake was first visited by a white person in 1875 when Canadian Pacific Railway surveyor Henry MacLeod travelled up the river from the Athabasca Valley and visited a place he called "Sorefoot Lake."

5 Schäffer, "The Valleys of the Saskatchewan with Horse and Camera," 41.

6 Schäffer, "The Infinite Variety of the Canadian Rockies," clipping.

7 Schäffer, "Teepee Life in the Northern Hills," 4.

8 Walter Wilcox, quoted in Gowan, "A Quaker in Buckskin," 2.

9 Schäffer, "Old Indian Trails: Expedition of 1907," in Hart, *A Hunter of Peace*, 16.

10 The official name of the mountain is Wilcox Peak but there is some confusion about this. That is the name suggested by Norman Collie in 1899 and it was officially approved by the Geographic Board of Canada in 1924. In 1928 the name was changed to Mount Wilcox, but in 1956 it was officially changed back again to Wilcox Peak. Search "Wilcox, Walter D." at Peakfinder, www.peakfinder.com/namedrop.asp (accessed March 6, 2011).

11 A "glissade" here refers to the voluntary act of descending a steep slope of snow in a controlled manner. It is in its simplest form a controlled slide on snow. There are three methods of glissading: the sitting glissade, the standing glissade and the crouching glissade. The one to use depends on snow and slope conditions, the appearance of runout and your mastery of the technique. Cox and Fulsaas, *Mountaineering*, 328.

12 Schäffer Warren to Minnie Nickell, November 12, [1936?], Minnie Nickell fonds, Whyte Museum of the Canadian Rockies, M493.

13 Warren, "The Heart of a Child," 2.

14 Hart, *A Hunter of Peace*, 81.

15 Ibid.

16 Ibid., 32.

17 "Essay on Pants," 8.

18 See Haweis, *The Art of Beauty*.

19 Photo titles in square brackets were composed by Whyte Museum archivists for images that were not titled.

20 Schäffer, *Old Indian Trails of the Canadian Rockies*, 204.

21 Hart, *A Hunter of Peace*, 35.

22 Schäffer Warren to Humphrey Toms, December 13, [1933?], Whyte Museum of the Canadian Rockies, M479/1, 3.

23 The spelling of Mary's maiden name as "Sharpless" appears to be interchangeable with the alternative "Sharples." I have consistently used "Sharpless" throughout the book, although Mary herself sometimes uses Sharples in her own writing (e.g., Schäffer Warren, "The Heart of a Child," 15).

24 Warren, "Palliser's Expedition, Some Intimate Glimpses," clipping.

25 Vaughan, *The Life and Work of Sir William Van Horne*, 151.

26 In Canada, the Big Bend is a northward arc of the Columbia River that runs through Big Bend Country in British Columbia, where the river leaves its initial northwestward course along the Rocky Mountain Trench to curve around the northern end of the Selkirk Mountains to head southeast between that range and the Monashees to the west.

27 Warren, "The Heart of a Child," 3.

28 Hart, *A Hunter of Peace*, 3.

29 Warren, "The Heart of a Child," 3.

30 Warren, "In the Heart of the Canadian Rockies with Horse and Camera, Part I," 9.

31 Treaty 7 was signed in 1877 between the Crown and southern Alberta First Nations, including the Nakoda (Stoney). This treaty led to the establishment of the reserve at Morley, near Banff, Alberta.

32 Warren, "The Heart of a Child," 3.

33 Schäffer, "Old Indian Trails: Expedition of 1907," in Hart, *A Hunter of Peace*, 71.

34 Warren, "The Heart of a Child," 4.

35 Ibid., 9.

36 Sanford Beck, *No Ordinary Woman*, 62.

37 Ibid., 62.

38 Warren, "The Heart of a Child," 50.

39 Hart, *A Hunter of Peace*, 2.

40 Warren, "In the Heart of the Canadian Rockies with Horse and Camera, Part II: At the Head Waters of the Saskatchewan and Athabaska: A Sequel to 'In the Heart of the Canadian Rockies,'" 1.

41 Schäffer, "Old Indian Trails: Expedition of 1907," in Hart, *A Hunter of Peace*, 16, 17.

42 Warren, "In the Heart of the Canadian Rockies with Horse and Camera, Part I," 2.

43 Search "Mount Rundle" at Peakfinder, www.peakfinder.com (accessed March 6, 2011).

44 Pierre Jean De Smet Papers. Washington State University Libraries, Pullman. Holdings listed at www.wsulibs.wsu.edu/masc/finders/cg537.htm (accessed March 6, 2011).

45 "White Man Pass." Search at www.peakfinder.com (accessed March 6, 2011).

46 Thrift, Gayle, "Captain John Palliser," Unpublished report for "Mavericks" permanent exhibit, Glenbow Museum, June 17, 2005, 1.

47 Warren, "Palliser's Expedition, Some Intimate Glimpses," clipping.

48 "In Memoriam: Arthur Philemon Coleman," 125.

49 Sanford and Sanford Beck, *Historic Hikes in Northern Yoho National Park*, 92.

50 Search "Habel, Jean" at Peakfinder, www.peakfinder.com/name-drop.asp (accessed March 6, 2011).

51 Habel, *The North Fork Valley of the Wapta (British Columbia)*.

52 Search "Mount Columbia" at Peakfinder, www.peakfinder.com (accessed March 6, 2011).

53 Schäffer Warren to Raymond Zilmer, February 29, 1928, Whyte Museum of the Canadian Rockies, M8/accn. 6081.

54 Schäffer, "Teepee Life in the Northern Hills," 5.

55 Ibid., 25.

56 Ibid., 23.

57 Schäffer, *Old Indian Trails of the Canadian Rockies,* 5.

58 Untitled clipping, *Banff Crag and Canyon,* May 30, 1908, 4.

59 Mollie Adams, quoted in Schäffer, *Old Indian Trails,* 232.

60 "To Again Visit Mountain Lake," *Edmonton Daily Bulletin,* June 5, 1911, 6.

61 Hart, *A Hunter of Peace,* 95.

62 Schäffer, "Locating and Measuring Lake Maligne," 3.

63 Sanford Beck, *No Ordinary Woman,* 107.

64 Throughout her text, Mary uses "Mt." as the abbreviation for the word "mount" in proper names and "mtn." as an abbreviation for the word "mountain" in general.

65 Lewis Swift, quoted in Mary T.S. Schäffer, *Old Indian Trails of the Canadian Rockies,* 117.

66 Hart, *A Hunter of Peace,* 118.

67 Ibid.

68 It is difficult to determine the origin of some of the buckskin clothing that belonged to Mary that is now in the Whyte Museum's collection. Makers are not identified.

69 Schäffer, *Old Indian Trails,* 328.

70 Ibid., 336–37.

71 Sanford Beck, *No Ordinary Woman,* 93.

72 Schäffer, "An American Boy in the Canadian Rockies," 1.

73 Schäffer Warren to Humphrey Toms, December 13, [1933?]. Whyte Museum of the Canadian Rockies, M479/I, 3.

74 Schäffer to George Vaux Jr., September 20, 1911. Whyte Museum of the Canadian Rockies, Vaux family fonds, M170, unprocessed file 3.

75 Mary Warren to Charles Reid, March 18, 1936. ACR, Charles Reid fonds, M413, file 2.

76 Gadd, *Bankhead,* 12.

77 Patton, *Parkways of the Canadian Rockies,* 13. The last record of a free-roaming bison in the Rockies was from 1858. It is estimated that a century earlier, between 30 and 60 million of these animals roamed this area. There is now a move afoot to return bison to the Bow Valley.

78 Warren, "In the Heart of the Canadian Rockies with Horse and Camera, Part I," 5.

79 Ibid., 215.

80 Krasner-Khait, "The Impact of Refrigeration."

81 Schäffer, "The Byways of Banff," 14.

82 Schriever, *Complete Self-Instructing Library of Practical Photography,* 1909.

83 This lantern slide projector was donated by Tom Lonsdale, but it likely belonged to Mary Schäffer.

84 "Lantern Slides Factsheet," *John Davidson – The Legacy of a Canadian Botanist.* UBC Botanical Garden and Centre for Plant Research, www.botanyjohn.org/en/learning-aids/lantern-slides (accessed March 8, 2011).

85 Elmendorf, *Lantern Slides,* 13, 14, 41, 42.

86 Panzer, *Philadelphia Naturalistic Photography, 1865–1906,* 6.

87 Schriever, *Complete Self-Instructing Library of Practical Photography,* 1016, 1025, 1027.

88 Warren, "In the Heart of the Canadian Rockies with Horse and Camera, Part I," 14.

89 Mary refers here to the Banff Springs Hotel, originally

completed by the Canadian Pacific Railway in 1888, now part of the Fairmont hotel chain.

90 Mary refers here to a small, naphtha-powered motor launch. *Naphtha* is the generic name for a number of different flammable-liquid mixtures of hydrocarbons that were used as fuels and solvents.

91 Because Mary was originally from the United States, I have retained her American spelling, e.g., color instead of colour.

92 The ten peaks were named by Samuel Allen, an early explorer of the region. His original list omitted Mount Hungabee but included Wenkchemna Peak, which is not as high as Hungabee and is really just an extension of it. See "Valley of the Ten Peaks," *Wikipedia*, http://en.wikipedia.org/wiki/Valley_of_the_Ten_Peaks, last modified January 30, 2011 (accessed March 6, 2011).

93 The accounts of both the 1907 and 1908 trips contain references to burnt timber. Also note that this slide shows Mollie Adams.

94 *Dough* is a slang term for money.

95 "The Ainu People." Ainu Museum, Hokkaido, www.ainu-museum.or.jp/en/study/eng01.html (accessed March 8, 2011). See also *Wikipedia*, http://en.wikipedia.org/wiki/Ainu (accessed July 27, 2010).

96 The date of the article is not known. See bibliography for full citation.

97 *Brigands* are gangs that ambush and rob people in forests and mountains.

98 A *queue* in this context is a long, braided ponytail that men wore at the back of their heads, not the British word for a line-up of people awaiting their turn.

99 *Kuruma* is the Japanese word for "car," but in this case, it more likely refers to a carriage, something that was pulled by horses or bikes or maybe people.

100 Schäffer, letter home, December 27, 1908, Whyte Museum of the Canadian Rockies, M79: 1, 12.

101 Schäffer, "Old Indian Trails: Expedition of 1907," in Hart, *A Hunter of Peace*, 80.

Batchelor, John. *The Ainu and Their Folk-Lore.* London: Religious Tract Society, 1901. Available online, www.archive.org/details/ainutheirfolkloroobatcrich (accessed March 8, 2011).

Beck, Janice Sanford. *No Ordinary Woman: The Story of Mary Schäffer Warren.* Calgary: Rocky Mountain Books, 2001.

Brown, Stewardson. *Alpine Flora of the Canadian Rocky Mountains.* Illustrated with watercolour drawings and photographs by Mrs. Charles Schäffer. New York: G.P. Putnam's Sons, 1907. Available online, www.archive.org/details/alpinefloraofcan-oobrowrich (accessed March 8, 2011).

Coleman, A.P. *The Canadian Rockies New and Old Trails.* Surrey, BC: Rocky Mountain Books, 2006. First published 1911 by T.F. Unwin.

Cox, Steven M., and Kris Fulsaas. *Mountaineering: The Freedom of the Hills.* 7th ed. Seattle: The Mountaineers Books, 2003.

Cullwick, Hannah, and Liz Stanley. *The Diaries of Hannah Cullwick, Victorian Maidservant.* (Douglass series on women's lives and the meaning of gender). First edition/first printing. Chicago: The Art Institute of Chicago and Olympic Marketing, 1984.

Elmendorf, Dwight Lathrop. *Lantern Slides: How To Make and Color Them.* New York: E. & H.T. Anthony & Co., 1895. Available online, www.archive.org/details/lanternslideshow-ooelmerich (accessed March 8, 2011).

Flanders, Judith. *The Victorian House.* New York: Harper Perennial, 2004.

Gadd, Ben. *Bankhead: The Twenty Year Town.* Calgary: Coal Association of Canada, in cooperation with Canadian Parks Service, 1989.

Gowan, Elsie Park. "A Quaker in Buckskin." *Alberta Historical Review* 5, no. 3 (Summer 1957): 2.

Habel, Jean. *The North Fork Valley of the Wapta (British Columbia).* N.p., 1898. Available online (scanned microform), www.archive.org/details/cihm_15172 (accessed March 8, 2011).

Hart, E.J. *A Hunter of Peace: Mary T.S. Schäffer's Old Indian Trails of the Canadian Rockies.* Banff: Whyte Museum of the Canadian Rockies, 1980.

Haweis, Mrs. H.R. *The Art of Beauty.* London: Chatto & Windus, 1883. Available online, www.archive.org/details/artofbeau-tyoohawe (accessed March 8, 2011).

"In Memoriam: Arthur Philemon Coleman," *Canadian Alpine Journal* 26 (1938): 125.

Krasner-Khait, Barbara, "The Impact of Refrigeration," *History Magazine*, February/March 2000, www.history-magazine.com/refrig.html; www.history-magazine.com/kk/back.htm (both accessed March 8, 2011).

MacColl, Gail, and Carol McD. Wallace. *To Marry an English Lord or, How Anglomania Really Got Started.* New York: Workman Publishing, 1989.

Morse, Edward S. *Japan Day by Day.* Atlanta, Ga.: Cherokee Publishing, 1990. First published 1917 by Houghton Mifflin Co..

Panzer, Mary. *Philadelphia Naturalistic Photography, 1865–1906: Yale University Art Gallery, New Haven, Connecticut, 10 February–7 April 1982*. New Haven, Conn.: The Gallery, 1982.

Patton, Brian. *Parkways of the Canadian Rockies: A Touring Guide to Banff, Jasper, Kootenay and Yoho National Parks*. 5th ed. Banff: Summerthought, 2008.

Sanford, Emerson, and Janice Sanford Beck. *Historic Hikes in Northern Yoho National Park*. Surrey, BC: Rocky Mountain Books, 2008.

Schäffer, Mary. "An American Boy in the Canadian Rockies." Unpublished MS. Whyte Museum of the Canadian Rockies, M79:4, 1912.

———. "Locating and Measuring Lake Maligne." Unpublished MS. Whyte Museum of the Canadian Rockies, M79: 3, n.d.

———. "Teepee Life in the Northern Hills." Unpublished MS. Whyte Museum of the Canadian Rockies, M79: 6, 1924.

Schäffer, Mary T.S. *Old Indian Trails of the Canadian Rockies*. Foreword by Janice Sanford Beck. Surrey, BC: Rocky Mountain Books, 2007. First published 1911 by G.P. Putnam.

———. "A Glimpse of the Head-hunters of Formosa," Unpublished MS, Whyte Museum of the Canadian Rockies, M79: 2, 1908.

Schäffer, Mrs. Charles, "The Infinite Variety of the Canadian Rockies," *Rod and Gun in Canada*. Clipping. Whyte Museum of the Canadian Rockies, M79, File 9A 751, n.d.

———. "The Valleys of the Saskatchewan with Horse and Camera," *The Bulletin of the Geographical Society of Philadelphia* 5 (April 1907): 108–114.

Schriever, J.B. *Complete Self-Instructing Library of Practical Photography*. 10 vols. Scranton, Pa.: American School of Art and Photography, 1909. Available online (search the title for links to all vols.), www.archive.org (accessed March 8, 2011).

Strasser, Susan. *Never Done: A History of American Housework*. New York: Owl Books, 2000.

Vaughan, Walter. *The Life and Work of Sir William Van Horne*. New York: Century, 1920. Available online, www.archive.org/details/lifeworkhorneoovaughanuoft (accessed March 8, 2011).

Warren, Mary S. "Palliser's Expedition, Some Intimate Glimpses." *Calgary Herald Supplement*. Clipping. Whyte Museum of the Canadian Rockies, M79, File 8, n.d.

———. "In the Heart of the Canadian Rockies with Horse and Camera, Part I." Unpublished lantern slide presentation. Whyte Museum of the Canadian Rockies, M7189/7, n.d., 9.

———. "The Byways of Banff." *Canadian Alpine Journal* 10 (1919): 78–91. MS held by Whyte Museum of the Canadian Rockies, M79: 5, n.d.

Warren, Mary Schäffer. "The Heart of a Child." Unpublished MS. Whyte Museum of the Canadian Rockies, M79 /7, 15.

———. "With the Hairy Ainus." *Travel and Exploration*. Clipping. Whyte Museum of the Canadian Rockies, M79:9A, n.d. See also "With the Hairy Ainus," *Travel and Exploration* 3 (1910): 377–84, reprinted in Kirsten Refsing, ed. *Early European Writings on Ainu Culture: Travelogues and Descriptions*, vol. IV. Tokyo: Edition Synapse, 2000.

Index

274

275